THE NEW ERA OF
CONSCIOUSNESS

THE NEW ERA OF
CONSCIOUSNESS

A Truly Transformative Journey Into Self-Healing,
Rejuvenation and ((Protection Energy))

JESSE ANSON DAWN

iUniverse, Inc.
Bloomington

The New Era of Consciousness
A Truly Transformative Journey Into Self-Healing, Rejuvenation and
((Protection Energy))

iUniverse books may be ordered through booksellers or by contacting:

iUniverse
1663 Liberty Drive
Bloomington, IN 47403
www.iuniverse.com
1-800-Authors (1-800-288-4677)

Because of the dynamic nature of the Internet, any web addresses or links contained in this book may have changed since publication and may no longer be valid. The views expressed in this work are solely those of the author and do not necessarily reflect the views of the publisher, and the publisher hereby disclaims any responsibility for them.

Any people depicted in stock imagery provided by Thinkstock are models, and such images are being used for illustrative purposes only.
Certain stock imagery © Thinkstock.

ISBN: 978-1-4759-7253-5 (sc)
ISBN: 978-1-4759-7275-7 (hc)
ISBN: 978-1-4759-7254-2 (ebk)

Library of Congress Control Number: 2013901362

Printed in the United States of America

iUniverse rev. date: 01/23/2013

CONTENTS

(((CHAPTER ONE)))

A GLOBAL NEW ERA DAWNS

"All love is based on language . . . voice its bones and
words its skin . . . love, like language, is a body . . . one
body. Yours."
—Tom Junod

"Let not authority be your truth, but let truth be your
authority."
—Herbert M. Shelton

Surely the time has come for us to **strongly** emphasize the
power of the written **word**, especially in regard to the fact that,
due to the immensely high cost of medical prescriptions and
procedures, the need for books about disease prevention is more
crucial than ever.

Therefore, as an author totally focused on truly effective,
cost-free ways to protect ourselves against illness, dwindling
vitality, and the various causes of aging, I have spent the last two
decades researching what is revealed in this long-labored piece
of work.

And although for many years, my previously written books
(**Never "Old"** and **The Rejuvenator's Bible**), have steadily sold
worldwide, it's clearly evident that what is now in (**your** hands)
is much more helpfully captivating than my earlier publications.

However, I do admit that in a world where "bigger is better"
has become a [TV world] obsession, a book is just a small thing.

But as we have seen, genuinely beneficial works of nonfiction can make very ((**BIG**)) improvements in people's lives, especially if they inspire new levels of well being. All while we realize that, quite essentially, a library is a hospital for the mind and body.

Thus by deeply appreciating the importance of that fact, I try to keep my books, magazine articles and songs duly focused on one significant aim:

To reveal techniques and discoveries that, quite comprehensively, reveal truly working methods of mind-over-body/self-renewal, whereby I continue to help humanity solve what seems to be:

Planet Earth's Biggest Mystery

Scientific studies have found that our bodies continually regenerate at a rate of about 150 million new cells a minute, a process that enables us to be completely repaired by our healing energy. But if that is basically true, then why does our immunity system, along with various body organs, steadily deteriorate with age?

All of which is a vastly unsolved, ongoing dilemma that brings to mind this momentous fact: according to international research, there is no medicine that can increase the longevity of physical regeneration, but it **can** be greatly sustained by merging psychology with several kinds of multifaceted techniques.

Therefore, to justifiably align with that vital piece of information, this book teaches a variety of ways to capably maximize self-restoration—methods that are both psychological and spiritual, along with dietary, musical and (and even humorous) ways to revitalize your brain and body.

But before entering the realm of truly effective, easily learned abilities that can initiate a new era of self-controlled healing, it helps to realize this:

Even in these modern times, a multitude of tests reveal that human mentality has learned to tap-into only a *(small percentage)* of its actual capacity. And that is a situation which I find difficult to ignore, especially since I've discovered how to potently direct the primary catalyst of physical repair—a body-revivifying, ((central-brain-emanation)) that is one of the principal themes of this unique book.

And yet, mainly because my extensive research has been unable to find an "official," medical industry name for what, quite apparently, is our (internal life-force), to clarify my perceptions and writings about it, I have come to call this ((surely significant)) phenomenon:

C.E. MINDPOWER

C.E. is an abbreviation for **Creational Energy**, and to take a glimpse at this fundamental essence of physical rejuvenation, simply (close your eyes), and take a few seconds to witness the dazzling sparkle of your C.E. Light . . . .

If you did this brief look into your (energy-body-((inner-self)), you may have noticed that it has a pulsating, electric-like vibrancy to it. Yes, it surely does, and due to my fervent belief in the powers of the healing luminosity (within us), along with my books and articles about its curative abilities, I've also released a CD of songs about what it can do, and here is a sample verse from that album:

I'm here to **relay** in my musical **way**—((**creational energy**)) that can truly **delay**—depressing doldrums of rapid decay—as step-by-step you can learn to **know**—how directed thought-waves make immunity **GROW**—via self-mending powers that cure illness and **pain**—helping you to be ((**totally healed again**)).

The title of that album is **The Omnipresent Urge**, and it's all about the endless desire for continuous health—a craving that, without a doubt, is as enduring as the dawning sun. And (hopefully), the compositions on that album will help people realize the importance of our ((brainpower-linked)), regenerative capacities, and thereby urge listeners to duly explore:

Willfully Aimed ((Mental Energy))

What you're now getting into goes far beyond fantasy or trivia, but instead this book reveals repeatedly proven ways to (inner-activate) **electro-genesis**, a process that the Webster's Collegiate Dictionary (quite briefly) defines as this: **"The production of electrolyte activity in living tissue."** And by thoroughly learning the ((self-renewing)) influence of that ability, we can gainfully utilize what has been, for far too long, perceived as merely a "mysterious enigma."

Thus along with my writings and CDs, to provide an alternative to vastly overpriced, mainly drug-linked healthcare, for nearly a decade now, I've been giving worldwide seminars that help people initiate their perpetually curing skills—well-attended gatherings firmly guided by what I call:

The Duo of Triumphant Truths

(1). **The most helpful parts of us are the immunity and regeneration systems, and the more we learn about the mind's ((glisteningly healing energy)), the more disease-free we will be, and the brighter we will shine.**

(2). **Due to the fallacy that people have very little control over our self-restoring powers, learning effective ways to maintain mental and physical renewal should, quite clearly, be our most precious human right.**

Therefore, duly motivated by that duo of truisms, my teachings stay steadily aimed at ways to stimulate the invaluable results of the increasingly developed, revivified mind. All of which is a process that, over time, encourages the need to give the TV a rest, because to capably activate (inner-visualized), life-saving skills, it highly depends on the mental freedom to learn about them. And it's via a [Tube-View]-free frame of mind that you may find the time to tune-into the **Body-Guardian-Genius-Channel**—the one ((**now**)) emerging (**inside**) **you**—the ((**enlightening**)) one that teaches us how:

Perceptions Create the Majority of Physical Effects

International studies find that **deeply** believing in one's self-curing powers is the most potent remedy of all. But to arouse that level of perception, whereby steadily caring about your body is not about "self-indulgence," but a vital way to survive, it truly helps to ask yourself ((willpower-sparking)) probes such as this:

Who is the **REAL** you? A "you" ruled by TV and pharmaceutical-pushed, [ageism-based] perceptions, or the revitalized **TRUE YOU** who, step-by-step, learns how to sustain your preciously needed, ((ongoing regeneration))? Otherwise, dear reader, if you let your restorative abilities fade away, you may fail to realize the **BIG** difference between initiating self-repair to ceaselessly happen, or just wondering **WHAT** the ?%#! **HAPPENED** to it? But fortunately, there are two future-world outcomes open to us: the world of "I wish I had" or the world of "I'm glad I did." And to help people transcend the ["I wish I had more time to learn about my body, where can I get a quick-fix?"] mode of thinking, I teach a gradually advancing, mind-expanding process that goes far beyond the merely temporary effects of chemical-based medications.

Yes, instead of relying on drugs, I've been exploring mind-powered remedies ever since 1967, back when I finished my "tour of duty" as a drafted soldier in Vietnam, an ordeal followed by four decades of searching this planet, seeking out examples of truly working, self-healing abilities.

Perhaps I could call that worldwide journey my Evolution of the Human Brain Tour, as between the ages of 23 and 65, I encountered so many prototypes of amazing body-control and agelessness, that I could do nothing less than publish information about what I have learned.

Thus my first effort to share the myriad of discoveries (revealed herein), was the 258-page book that I called Never "Old"—the one chosen to be the winner of the N.A.I.P. (National Association of Independent Publishers) Content Award in 1993.

And then, soon after winning that honor, came the launching of my Never "Old" column, a feature that, since 1994, has been running in the Los Angeles based, Awareness magazine—a publication that usually contains articles written by some of the most famous authors on this planet.

(Note): Along with its printed circulation to over 100,000 readers (a number that is rapidly growing), Awareness is also available online. And if you want to read about my latest mind-over-body findings, simply go to awarenessmag.com on the internet, and there, at that ((knowledge-expanding)) website, you'll find my column in the Current Issue/Departments section.

And thanks to the popularity of my Awareness articles, I get featured as a Whole Life Expo, keynote speaker at their huge events throughout the U.S., the largest of which is held at the Las Vegas Convention Center. And so after decades of dues-paying research—"suddenly" I've been launched into being an "overnight sensation"—a "New Age Hit" in "Big Time" Vegas!

But of course, unlike the "stars" of the entertainment media, the importance of a nonfiction author is not based simply on physical attractiveness, but it's mainly about the knowledge ((vitally)) contained within our brains.

However, as to the results of mind-over-body abilities, surely it starts when we are born, a process clearly revealed by my 1-year-"old" son. For example, if he's feeling good, he creates what I call the Original Grin, but when he cries, he evokes the [[instant-aging]] influence of negative emotions, as suddenly his flawless face gets fiercely wrinkled, giving him the look of a toothless old man. Wow, what a stunning display of ((thought-waves)) **RULING** the body, and how quickly moods can shift, from happy to sad and then back to joyful again, all while he wails the sounds that get him fed, plus the comfort of being touched.

Also, his somewhat alarmingly loud, vocal outbursts keep teaching me a prominent fact: mind-emanated, positive energy causes vastly different physical effects than negative energy—a crucial realization that can last a lifetime. And it all generates from one place: the center of the human brain.

Therefore, by firmly believing in the ((positive-energy-healing-thoughts)) process, despite reaching the [65+], so-called "retired" phase of my life, I continue to embody the look and vitality of a "normal" 29 or 30—just as the recent photo of me (on this book) **accurately** verifies. Yes, that's the **REAL** me at age 68, and that's my **real** hair, and my **surgery-free, make-up-free, real** face. And you can be quite **sure** of that, because nothing is faked or deceptive about my regeneration-reviving techniques, mainly because I perceptively **LIVE** via this enduringly helpful truism: **rejuvenation is both a physical and deeply MENTAL process.**

Thus by potently ((internalizing)) that fact, I have, quite naturally, kept nearly the same face and body for almost 40 years—a result that often urges people to ask me this: "How **long** can your methods keep working so **well**?" And my truly honest reply is this: mental energy ((**steadily**)) heals, but its ongoing ability strongly depends on not falling into what I call:

The Skeptic Tank

The way I see it, the Skeptic Tank is a mode of [mind and body defeating], cynical negativity that, to a large extent, is spurred by the (long promoted) notion that self-empowered, curative abilities are not "scientifically established." But if all of "science" is based on actual reality, then bumblebees couldn't fly, because "scientifically" its wings are too small to lift its body. And yet bumblebees ((positively)) launch themselves anyway—a marvelous talent that I too would love to have the wings to do. But sometimes, after seeing the truly transformative results of my self-renewing methods, I feel like I'm ((**mindfully**)) flying, especially when realizing how successfully I've overcome what I call:

The [Old Era] System

And I will now explain how that [[backwards-thinking]], antiquated system of so-called "curing" can be momentously improved.

The [Old Era] System, although hugely profitable, is a conglomeration of overly toxic [and too often ineffective] procedures that began during what I call the coldly complacent, **BRR** period (**B**efore my **R**ejuvenation **R**evolution).

BRR indeed, so chillingly anti-progress is the [Old Era] of healthcare that, for the most part, its practitioners have used only scalpels and [side-effect-loaded] drugs to perform their business. All while ignoring safer (and much more effective) methods such as healing-oriented hypnosis, along with mind-over-body, self-curing massage and holism, techniques that most physicians stubbornly disregard, mainly due to the claim that dietary and surgery-free approaches are "not successfully instituted." But as to the notion that medical "success" is all about making piles of money, when it comes to actually **curing** diseases, strictly "standard" methods, far too frequently, fill up the cemeteries

All of which is a [[[stuck-in-reverse] dilemma that reminds me of this sarcastic riddle: How many [Old Era] doctors does it take to change a burned-out light? None. Because they fear any changes that can limit their cash-flow.

But instead of fearing change, the time has come to change our concept of fear, because OVERCOMING the [Old Era] dread of a burgeoning New Era of preventive ways of self-curing is, quite clearly, a vitally needed advancement. Thus it's becoming increasingly certain that humanity will soon awaken, gather together and **DEMAND** the following urgently needed change:

A **GLOBAL** movement of conscientious healthcare reforms—truly ethical reforms that foster a newly **affordable,** thoroughly re-**humanized** system—one that will, first of all, enact more regulations over what's become known as:

The Ever-Ballooning, "Big Pharma" Problem

"Big Pharma" is the satirical name given to this planet's most profitable business—pharmaceuticals—a cartel that has discovered (or invented?) so many diseases, that they now sell more than 15,000 kinds of chemical-based "medications," all of which adds up to profits of over $500 billion a year.

As "Big Pharma's" pill-popping craze has fully phased-out the "good old days," back when medicine cabinets contained maybe some aspirin and Alka-seltzer. But now, throughout this increasingly chemo-hooked planet, people commonly take risky drugs (such as antidepressants and anti-cholesterol capsules, along with diuretics). And although these pills induce side effects that, far too often, cause heart attacks and kidney failure, nevertheless, these chemical-lab concoctions continue to nearly **double** their annual profits.

For example, there is the (rarely lethal) "perk-you-up" potion—Prozac—a pill that rakes in more cash than industry giants such as the Ford Corporation (a stunning fact about "priorities"). Woo-ha!—Prozac—the potent pop-scription so pervasive that I heard a comedian joke about a "pharmacy action film" coming out—a "drugstore cowboy thriller" called "Get Me My Prozac!"

Further yet, another sarcastic scheme for a film about Prozac was that of the zany comic who calls himself "The Nutty Movie Maker"—he whose "jest for the health of it" idea for a documentary was this: He, along with a camera crew, would take a box filled with 100 Prozac-fed hamsters to the Netherlands city of Amsterdam. And there they would set this dizzied mob of critters free to roam the streets, all while they filmed a movie about them called **"Hamsterdam."**

Ah yes, laughter **IS** good medicine, but surely it's no joke that "happiness" has massively become a drug-activated feeling—a [mind-controlling] concept mainly induced by "Big Pharma" Power and TV ads that sell various, so-called "remedies." But of course, a central goal of television is to sell products, an obligation that has its deepest influence during the 7 to 9 pm "primetime," when the [Tube-View] makes us quickly drowsy, the ideal time to push pills, plus lots of chemical-loaded "soft drinks" and junk food.

And yet even though I occasionally watch TV, when a barrage of annoyingly phony advertisements come on, I often mute the "telly" and switch-on one of my ((Wake-Me-Up)) songs—self-empowering little ditties such as the one I call:

Beyond Chemomania

I pay no heed to cola jingles, and TV-pushed "medications"—
All of those "Big Pharma" ploys, aiming for a drug-laced nation—

And to keep my brain and body from getting too impaired—
I switch on some music, whenever commercials get aired—
As more and more I find, that TV is just "killing" time,
So I don't let it rule me, and damage my health and
mind . . .

Also, I **refuse** to let television eliminate book reading
from my life, especially truly helpful non-fiction, because the
((personal-revolution)) of activated-mind-power is far too
essential to let it fade away, steadily numbed by overdoses of
TV-addicted, body and brain drainage.

But regardless of the ads that constantly push [secretly
harmful] potions and lotions, of course I **do** realize that **some**
pharmaceuticals can be safely beneficial, especially those well
established as being non-toxic and genuinely effective.

However, as for doctor-prescribed medicines, according
a book called "**The Longevity Revolution**" (a brilliant
piece of work written by the Pulitzer Prize winning author,
Dr. Robert N. Butler), he highly recommends that, before
taking a personally untested drug, "**always** read the list of its
possible side-effects." And during this time of widely marketed,
increasingly dangerous pills, that is a very important piece of
advice, especially in light of this potentially ((life-saving)) fact:

**According to recently reported, worldwide studies,
allergic reactions to pharmaceuticals are now the fourth
leading cause of death.**

But regardless of that long-hidden statistic, to avoid any
government efforts to address the problem of frequently lethal
medications, pharmaceutical firms easily spend **billions** of
dollars to keep politicians firmly in their pocket.

And yet almost as ((financially expanding)) as Big Pharma's
relentlessly pushed Pill-Parade-Power, there is:

The Steadily Spreading ((Surge)) of Surgery

Extensive studies show that between 2008 and 2012, the amount of surgical procedures being done has **doubled**, especially since "cosmetic" operations have become so widely popular. Although be aware that "facelifts" are only a temporary "fix," mainly due to this thoroughly proven fact:

In the same way that a rubber band weakens after being ceaselessly strrrretched, skin-tightening surgery usually only lasts between three and six months, because the extended skin tends to loosen-up again, thereby requiring another costly, stretch-and-re-stitch operation.

Therefore, much to the delight of the cosmetic surgeon, the short-lived effects of "face-lifting" tend to create a continually returning customer—all while [totally unregulated] surgical fees (especially in the U.S.), keep rising higher and higher.

But dear reader, my intentions are not meant to belittle people who try the cosmetic surgery approach to rejuvenation, because my goal is to provide valid alternatives that are self-empowering and costless. For example, I highly recommend trying out the ((perpetually effective)), **You-nity Self-Massage** methods, or the **Inner Directions** techniques (all of which are truly helpful procedures clearly detailed in Chapter 2 of this book). And yet for now, let me again provide a verse from one of my ((hopefully uplifting)) songs—a bit of surgery-sarcasm that I call:

Learning to Lose the Face-Sagging Blues

So many people paying big bucks dues,
to erase wrinkles that they hope to lose,
paying huge chunks of their hard-earned riches,
to get faces stretched with scalpels and stitches,

and after getting a series of tucks and snips,
will it make people start to blink their lips?
But instead paying for what surgeons can do,
I use my **cost-free** ways to ((**SELF**-renew)) . . .

Yes indeed, as by energizing the truly rejuvenating methods
(revealed herein), facial surgery then becomes merely one of two
choices: **Choice One**: An increasingly expensive amount of
"facelifts." Or **Choice Two**: Learning how to utilize both
physical and ((psychologically induced)) methods that, if done
with due perseverance, are quite effective. Or as the Eleanor
Roosevelt wisely put it: "Beautiful youngsters are works of
Nature, but beautiful old people are *self*-created works of art."

And speaking of artfully, self-designing abilities, long ago
I was strongly inspired by a classic book about that subject,
a volume written by Dr. Maxwell Maltz, a well established
cosmetic surgeon who, quite famously, gave up surgery to
write psychology books. And in this quote from his best-seller,
"**Psycho-Cybernetics**," Dr. Maltz explains why he decided to
change careers:

"While doing research for this book, I came upon this
monumental fact: by persistently giving oneself deeply
felt, physically-healing directions, a penetrating form of
mentally-induced energy can, if willfully focused, heal (and
thereby rejuvenate) bodies more permanently than surgery."

And although Maltz's claims drew criticism from
many plastic surgeons, his **Psycho-Cybernetics** became an
international sensation, in which he says this:

"Any breakthrough in science is 1 likely to come from
outside the system." And then Maltz points out that: "Pasteur
was no M.D., the Wright brothers not aviators but bicycle
mechanics, and Einstein was not a physicist when turning
the physics world upside-down, while Nobel Prize winner,
(longtime physicist) Madam Curie, acquired her worldwide
fame in the medical field."

Then along came Maxwell Maltz, a famous surgeon who, via the teachings of his **Psycho-Cybernetics**, made vital changes amid the field of psychology—a classic book that made me realize that the mind-over-body process truly **IS**:

The New Wave of Human Evolution

And to help me ride this New Era wave of "age"-defying evolution, I have developed my **SAFE-"T"** ((Self-Affirming/ Freely-Evolving "Time")) process. For example, a **SAFE-"T"** way of thinking is to, quite persistently avoid the belief that "time is money," because that concept mainly applies to business world paychecks. But within the (reality check) of **YOUR** body, time is **not** money it is ((**LIFE**)), because one's precious heart can never pump cash, but if not [overly pressured], it can greatly help to **KEEP** you self-renewing and **alive**.

Or as Henry Miller's brilliant book called "**The Wisdom of the Heart**" put it: "**Imagine having all the time that you need to duly fulfill your destiny.**"

And after forty years of research, it seems that my true destiny is to teach, evident by the steady stream of people coming to my seminars—the week-end classes that I give in my backyard—a serene place that shoulders a splendid, seaside cove, nicely nestled on the east coast of Hawaii Island.

And it's amid my little slice of Hawaiian paradise that, for over a decade, I've been sharing my Creational Energy system of self-healing—techniques that draw in people from all over the U.S. (and also Europe). And as to why they come from near and far, just to learn from "Youthman Messenger" Jesse, perhaps it's largely due to an increasing interest in what my brochure calls:

The Three Pillars of Crucial Education

(1). Deeply learning that happiness is basically an (**inside job**), and the **real** measure of wealth is not money, but health, vitality, and healing knowledge.

(2). Thoroughly realizing that we cannot solve our problems with the same thinking that created them—a truism that helps us face the fact that, during every minute that we are depressed or ill, we lose a minute of enlightenment.

(3). Perceptively grasping that mind-power, if expanded beyond [ageism-based] notions, can take us to vastly new levels of vibrantly lived longevity.

And it's these three guidelines that keep my open-forum style, seaside sessions firmly aimed at teaching people about what has come to be known as:

Medical Ageism

Basically, medical ageism is a well-established, profit-based belief-system that, for several decades, has been widely initiated by the following, so-called "scientific truth."

"Once we reach the falling apart, verging on senility age of 65, we should not only retire from working, but to reach the [normal life expectancy] of 75, we should put ourselves steadily under a doctor's care."

Oh really? But I see that as a blatantly ageist ploy to keep us controlled by an unfairly overpriced, medical industry, all while we stay continuously [uneducated] about ways to effectively self-repair and regenerate our bodies.

And yet via my so-called "non medical," (cutting-"aging"-in-half) system, I have truly self-induced the appearance and vitality of 34 (or less) at 68 years "old," whereby I'm fearlessly looking forward to becoming at least 100. Why? Because if I reach the highly regarded goal of living more than a century, at that time, I will probably look and feel like no more than 50, a result that will clearly dispel any doubts about the procedures that I do and teach. All of which reveals the fact that stimulated regeneration is not about being able to pay for it, but more so about **developing** what is (**within** us), a vast amount of ((healing-energy)) that, in the long run, is greatly helped by the power of **H.O.P.E.** (**H**aving **O**nly **P**ositive **E**xpectations).

And a good example of that progressively uplifting mentality, is fellow anti-ageism activist Morris Rocklin, an intensely alive centenarian who recently experienced this noteworthy incident:

A week after Morris turned a feisty 101, he visited a doctor to get some advice about a lingering pain in his right knee. And after that physician gave his ailing leg a thorough examination, he told Morris basically this:

"Well sir, I don't detect any muscle or bone damage. But of course, it's quite normal for elderly folks like you to have . . . ongoing pains in your body."

But being the ((("defiant survivor"))) that Morris is, he indignantly replied: "Okay doc, so if painful ailments are supposedly . . . typical at my age, then why is my **right** knee aching, but my **left** knee always feels **fine**? Is it because most physical problems come from a lack of mental focus on body-symmetry?" And **that** was a vital discovery which "Mighty Morris" soon shared with me, a relatively unknown, self-healing method that I will now make public:

When you experience pain that is only on one side of you, there is a ((curative-energy)) way to alleviate it, simply by doing what I call **Mindpower-Massage/Mirror-Imaging.** This is a process that maximizes the natural urge to massage away aches, doing so by willfully directing your (regenerative thought-waves) to flow from the pain-free side over to its other-half—the pain-injured side—all while repeatedly (inner-voicing) the words **"balance now, heal now."**

And if that invocation is done with **steady determination**, it enables you to ((**energy-equalize**)) your system (((-)))—a method that I (along with many of my students), have found to be an effectively healing ailment-reliever. However, keep in mind that self-repair greatly depends on **BELIEVING** in its potency, whereby we activate what II call ((**Willfully-Focused-Connectivity**)).

All of which is an inborn process that begins in the mother's womb, where each doubled-up part of us forms a ((lifelong-healing-link)) with its (other-half).

Thus we come to realize that ((thought-projection)) is not a far-fetched concept, especially during these "cyberspace" times when, via ((wave-lengths)) generated from a computer, healing messages can be sent vast distances.

And speaking of the worldwide-web, quite unlike television, amid which "info" flashes by too fast to be studied, via the myriad of health information now available from various websites, knowledge about our bodies can be expanded **far** beyond the "sound-bites" of the [TV] world. Also, the internet urges us to ((**READ**)), whereby we can install newly helpful "software" into our brains.

For example, just to see what it would say about it, recently I typed the word "ageism" in the Wikipedia.org search window, whereby I found this clearly revealing, comprehensive paragraph about this [rarely mentioned on TV] topic—a brief (but memorable) piece that said this:

"**Ageism** profoundly affects both the elderly and the young, because after being steadily stereotyped as 'uselessly unproductive kids,' or worse yet, 'weakly decrepit and unemployable,' so-called 'old folks,' this portrayal usually becomes a self-fulfilling prophecy."

Then, after reading that, what came to mind were the supposedly "useless delinquents" who I "hung out" with in high school, most of whom, largely due to the effects of violent movies, would often get into fights, a reckless attitude that I too was (reluctantly) drawn into.

But thankfully, during my first year of college, my mother gave me a fascinating book written by Alan Watts, his classic piece of work titled "**The Supreme Identity.**" And it was that highly conscious, perception-expanding volume that inspired me to read one psychology-oriented, nonfiction author after another, whereby I have advanced onto a more beneficially educated, self-enabling way of life. And of course, unlike the internet (which requires a fee to use it), once a good book is bought, it's good for a lifetime, free of charge.

And speaking of brilliantly influential writers, in 1983 (when I was 39), I read "**An Open Book**"—an unforgettably captivating piece of work written by the legendary movie director/author/script-writer, John Huston. But soon after reading that, I heard the sad news that he was dying from a very serious case of emphysema. And because I was totally transfixed by his vibrant style of writing, I wrote him a letter, telling Mr. Huston that perhaps I could revitalize his health, mainly by administering one of my Massage-and-Talk sessions**.**

And then, several days later, to my surprise, he called me, asking if I could come to his house, apparently anxious to see what I could do for him.

But when I emanated my (physical-plus-psychological) massage onto the body of the 76 year-old John Huston, I explained that this process involves defying the profit-based, medical industry ploy that fosters the notion that our disease-resisting, self-curing powers are very weak.

Nevertheless, although **three doctors** told Mr. Houston that he had only a "few months" to live, perhaps my ((self-healing-arousing)) method helped him, because soon after I urged his mind to merge with his body, he evoked a so-called "miraculous recovery," whereby he lived four more years. And they were truly **vibrant** years, during which he wrote and directed more good movies, with the second of his (doctor-predicted, "post death") films winning his daughter Angelica an Oscar, while it also got John nominated for Best Director.

True story! And also a good example of the ((illness-subduing)) benefits of not [jumping-to-conclusions], a habit that, far too often, is part of the "standard procedure" of medical practices.

But the way I see it, so-called "miraculous recoveries" go far beyond what biological teachings have come to call "our basic five senses"—the abilities of seeing, hearing, touching, smelling and tasting. All of which are, quite naturally, wonderful faculties that help us be fully functioning beings. And yet I have found that, unless we learn to perceptively focus on the (**here and now**) of our sensory capabilities, their life-enhancing powers gradually diminish. Why? Mainly because we can only see, hear, touch, smell or taste something that happens within (**the present time**), but if we're too often distracted by memories of the past, (present-time-sensory-awareness) decreases.

Also, along with developing the (in-the-moment) nature of our fundamental senses, I strongly emphasize the importance of what I perceive as our **Sixth Sense**—a truly significant blessing that I call **The Sense of Focused Healing.** And of course, if that essential empowerment weakens, diseases can quickly overtake us, especially if we are kept from being duly educated about ways to effectively arouse our self-repairing, regenerative systems.

Also, we deeply depend on what could be called our **Seventh Sense**—the vital skill that directs all physical actions, without which, even driving a car would be too dangerous, because even a brief loss of controlling a vehicle could cause fatal injuries. But fortunately, we have a ((muscle-movement-commanding)) sense that can control the speed of motorized "horsepower" with ((brainpower)), and so I call our ((safe-guarding)) seventh sense—**The Sense of Continual Body-Management.**

Thus by comprehending the (((speed-of-light))) energy of the ["officially" unnamed] sixth and seventh senses, perhaps we can develop a level of consciousness that, if vividly perceived, can uplift our sensory perceptions into newly expanded capabilities.

And with that significant aim in mind, I often wonder why (fourth-dimensional-healing-energy) courses aren't taught in medical schools, whereby physicians could, quite helpfully, receive a diploma that requires learning about methods of ((brain-energized)), self-curing.

All of which is a [long overlooked] need that reminds me of a former holder of many highly honored medical degrees, Dr. Stuart Berger, author of the runaway best-seller—**"Forever Young"**—an "anti-aging" book published when he was only 40 years old. But sadly, probably because his methods were mainly [chemical-formula-based] and not ((mind-powered/ sensory-oriented)), Dr. Berger never made it to age 41, because a few months after **"Forever Young"** was launched, he passed on from an apparent "heart attack."

Although whatever caused Dr. Berger's early demise, he was one of the many examples pointed out in a fascinating article written by the **Nobel Prize** nominee, Dr. Joel Wallach—a startling piece titled: "**Learn Why the Average Life Span of a M.D. is Only 58 years.**"

Dr. Wallach, a world renowned expert in the field of human longevity, is an intrepid opponent of "customary" (but consistently ineffective) medical practices. And according to Dr. Wallach's extensive research, the main reason why commonly futile procedures keep getting used, is largely because they are firmly established in what he calls "the locked-box of outdated medical credentials." Ah yes, "essential credentials" via [Old Era], unsharpened pencils (that have lost their point)—but amid the healing realm, medical degrees have little or nothing to do with what could be recognized as our **Eighth Sense**—a truly benevolent ability that I've recently come to call:

The Sense of Compassion

Quite unfortunately, ways to develop deeper levels of sympathy are not part of the conventional medical school teachings, but it's a way of thinking usually evoked by people gifted with a remarkable concern for the well being of humanity. For example, much of this planet has heard about the warmhearted wisdom of the South African, people-liberator Nelson Mandela, the ((busily-alive-and-well-at-94+)), true humanitarian who is often quoted as saying this:

"If we learn to activate the resonating harmony that shines from our souls, we can overcome the hatred-based disease of racism, whereby we realize that all races are equal in the eyes of God the Creator."

Thus by communicating his world-famous sense of compassion, Nelson Mandela represents the rare talent of linking consciousness and truth unforgettably together, a truly special person who, again and again, has helped to renew our faith in the spoken and written word.

But as for the healing-messages of "health-writers" like me, unfortunately, it's become mainly a cliché-ridden, doctor's club of usually unskilled authors who, for the most part, never **really** explored the depths of ((worldwide-visionary)), word-dynamics. For in truth, the strictly three-dimensional, medical industry is conventionally [shortsighted], especially when it comes to:

Our Life-Saving Abilities of Choice

After listening to a tape recording of a seminar that I gave at the Los Angeles Hilton, I was again inspired by hearing what a woman in the audience said, especially when she mentioned the potentials of a steadily educated way of life, a very motivating comment that stated this:

"I'm so thankful that I've chosen to embrace the learning process, as by reading your books, I've **finally** taken the time to study about what **really** matters, the healing powers of my mind and spirit. And by being here today, I can already feel that my ability to overcome self-destruction has become stronger, as I now realize that, to benefit from truly helpful knowledge, we must take the first step toward learning it, even when we have yet to see the whole staircase."

Thus it's not surprising that I cherish the recording of that woman's heartfelt words. As here was someone who, after announcing to the audience there that she is "98 years young," due to her cheerfulness and open-minded intelligence, she represented a memorable example of someone focused on the bright side of life—the dimension where it's not too dark to read. All while she has obviously avoided the [ageism-based] notion steadily promoted by TV shows, a mode of programming that, all too often, portrays "senior citizens" as absent-minded, grumpy people who exhibit what has come to be called:

"Natural Senescence"

According to research done by various pharmaceutical research labs, "natural senescence" has become the standard term for the supposedly "automatic" degeneration of human brain-cells—a malady that's been widely publicized as being "unavoidable without medication."

But if the truth be told, these "inescapably senile" claims are largely spurred by drug companies "culturing" human brain-cells in laboratory glassware, whereby these cells are ***totally disconnected* from the brain's self-renewing energy**. All of which is like testing to see if an electric-powered device can somehow function, even when unplugged from its power source!

Yes, as greedily illegitimate as that may seem to be, that's actually what these self-serving experiments try to do. And so when it comes to believing in the profit-based claims of "Big Pharma," keep in mind that it's a lot like trusting hungry dogs to guard a plate of hamburgers.

However, as to what has been actually **proven** about the longevity of brain cells, the following statement comes from a scientist **not** employed by a drug company, the eminent Dr.

Alexis Carrel, the brilliant **Nobel Prize** winner (briefly quoted here in his **Nobel** acceptance speech):

> **"Amid the natural process of regeneration, if human brain cells are continually supplied with the mental energy that enables them to steadily activate cellular restoration, as far as we know, total body renewal can last for an unlimited, yet to be discovered amount of time."**

Therefore, a fully functioning, keenly perceptive longevity is far more attainable than what "natural senescence" theorists lead us to believe, especially in light of the fact that, just as bodies need exercise to stay healthy, our brains need mental stimulation to continually regenerate. And according to extensive research about the "use-it-or-lose-it, sink-or-swim" process of mind-activation, nothing is more mentally empowering than reading earnestly truthful, deeply insightful authors of self-help nonfiction.

And yet, perhaps even songs can help to keep our "thinking caps" actively aware, especially if they contain crucial information. For example, to shed some light on the globally important subjects of senility, medical ageism and overly dangerous medications, I've recorded CD albums that contain songs that tell the truth about these increasingly deceptive, healthcare dilemmas.

But being the "late-bloomer" that I am, I didn't begin recording my songs until I felt **truly** ready, and after getting together with some of Hawaii's best musicians, I released my first healthcare-oriented album at the age of 62. And here is sample verse from the CD that I call **Mind-Over-Body Revelations**—a feisty little spiel titled:

Believe In What Is REAL

In order to sell millions of pills, they publish a phony story,
claiming that brain-cells get "senile," when tested in a
   laboratory.
But if their lab-tested cells degenerate, and steadily fade
   away,
cut off from mind-power **energy**, no **wonder** those cells
   decay.
But to profit from their "dying" cells claim, they've got a
   brand new pill,
so should we quickly buy that drug, so that our brain-cells
   don't get ill?
Or is it just a fabrication, a ploy to push their latest
   medication?
But I'm here to teach a **better way—self-renewing**
   EDUCATION . . .

Yes indeed, that's **MY** style of song-writing, and yet it's
no surprise that lyrics about self-curing are not "top 40,"
radio-gaga material. Nevertheless, I continue trying to
transcend the deluge of pop-tart-songs, mainly via compositions
aimed at a self-healing cause (and not just sexually excited
applause)—songs that generate a consciousness that overcomes
ageist adages such as this one: "Old dogs" (or old people?) "can't
learn new tricks."

And of course, for various "practical" reasons, "big hit"
songs stay boringly aligned with this [refusing to be educated]
attitude: "Just keep feeding me eye-candy, and don't make me
think too much."

But my goal is to go **BEYOND** that mentally
[[wheel-spinning]] [frame of mind], mainly by getting
progressively aware of insights based on ((brainpower))—a
process helpfully clarified by the important biological
declaration that has come to be called:

The First Law

The First Law (of Thermodynamics) is summed up by this quote from a somewhat uniquely advanced, college-level textbook called "Biology: A Human Approach," wherein this monumental Law of Nature is stated as basically this:

> **"If reactivated by the mind-power that keeps them functioning, brain cells will continue to swiftly heal the body that they live in and regenerate. But if mental stimulation is allowed to steadily decrease, thought-emanated abilities will surely fade away."**

But far be it from the pharmaceutical industry to let scientific facts prevent them from raking-in billions of dollars selling pills that supposedly counteract the "brain-cell decay" that causes "senility." All of which lines up with the medication-mania system that, mainly due to Big Pharma's hugely promoting, media-controlling budget, so-called "wonder drugs" get massively publicized, even though the advertisers {{pushing these pills}} fail to know if they really work.

Typical was the Time magazine cover story titled **"The Scientific Search for Ways to Keep Us FOREVER YOUNG"**—surely an eye-grabbing article, but filled with the same DNA-tweaking double-talk that's been around for decades. And yet despite the endless rehash of what I call ad-"news," during my forty+ years of paying close attention to publicized "medical breakthroughs," I've yet to find one supposedly "anti-aging" drug that is genuinely newsworthy.

In fact, when it comes to discoveries that would significantly extend human longevity, according to well-researched medical statistics, during the past decade, **the United States has slipped from 11th place to 48th place in worldwide life-expectancy!** So where is the "new progress" in that?

"Progress"-bogged-guess—**HELLO**! It's **New Era TIME—THE** time for mind-over-body psychology to advance to the forefront of the healthcare industry, despite the fact that nearly every "medical news" report is focused on the advertiser's new pills.

But regardless of pharmacology ploys to stifle a new era of self-enabled longevity, I believe that by reading crucially informative books (such as this one), humanity will soon direct more attention toward answering [too long overlooked], life-versus-death questions such as this:

HAS ANYONE EVER DIED OF "OLD AGE?"

According to international research, most elderly people perish from what is called "natural causes"—a term commonly used to label the death of "old folks" who, after being examined, were not clearly afflicted with a nameable disease. Therefore, to somehow (categorize) this very frequent situation, unexplainable fatalities are said to be "naturally" caused by an "age"-based loss of basic bodily functions.

But I'm a firm disbeliever in the vague and rather shortsighted "natural causes" notion, because I see it as a way to excuse [Old Era] methods that fail to prevent, diagnose or cure the second largest cause of death: the probably diet-related, "mutated cells" that cause cancer.

However, largely due to the ongoing inability to detect what goes on inside us, the "natural causes" term can ("conveniently") handle the paperwork involved with labeling the "mysteriously" deceased.

As I again emphasize that a vibrantly alive, disease-conquering life is mainly a matter of how deeply we perceive (and thereby energize) the development of the basic building blocks of our bodies. And a good (first step) toward a truly comprehensive understanding of our inborn, life-sustaining components is to declare:

A Better Name for "Cells"

Quite often I wonder how our endlessly re-creating, ((internal regenerators)) came to be called ["cells"]—a label that brings to mind tiny jail cells, where prisoners sit locked-up, rotting away in continuous depression.

Thus due to the fact that what we label things tends to affect our basic conception of them, instead of perceiving our ((ever-renewing)) body-units as vaguely connected ["cells"], I prefer to respectfully distinguish them as being **Perpetual-Life-Clusters.** Yes, that name sounds much less [boxed-in] than "cells" to me, and so be it as understood between us.

Okay then, moving progressively forward, let us now re-examine another problematic, rather twisted term for the unceasing creation of life—that which is clumsily called—

The "Big Bang" Theory

If we think about it, whoever named the origin of life on ((lovely Mother Earth)) as merely a yahoo-violent, [[["**Big Bang!**"]]] explosion, must have been a military strategist, or a producer of combat movies. Okay, sure, I realize that, for various reasons, we get programmed to be wowed by things that go **Ka-BOOM!**—but let us intelligently **rethink** foolishly, war-pushing notions I say, especially when it comes to nurturing ((**ever-evolving creation**)). Or as the life-affirming, Dr. "New Dimensions" Deepak Chopra wisely said: "Real awareness of natural origination focuses on artistic design, and not violent fragmentation."

Therefore, to align with the persistently clarifying aims of this book, I prefer to change the name "Big Bang Theory" to **The Creational Energy Theory** instead, because only a brilliantly creative intelligence could have originated the awesome beauty of unspoiled Nature. Indeed, just imagine the amount of ingenious artistry it takes to conceive the extremely beautiful intricacy of a rainforest, or the multicolored array of beings in the oceans—none of which look like they were formed by a brainlessly, bomb-like, destructive explosion.

All of which points to fact that perpetual life stems from conscious creativity and not blindly destructive forces. Thus by steadily activating the ever-renewing powers (within us), we can overcome the self-destructive belief that "aging" is a process that "cannot," in any way, be subdued by the abilities of one's mind.

And yet recently I read a somewhat [anti-brainpower] book that tries to establish what the author calls "The Law of Natural Decay"—a controversial piece of work written by cellular biologist, Leonard Hayflick—a volume titled **"How and Why We Age."**

In that obviously [Old Era]-based book, the author's principal theme is what he calls "Hayflick's Limit." And what that entails is, yet another theory derived from laboratory-tested cells of human brain tissue, whereby Hayflick's experiments supposedly indicate that, due to "unavoidably" withering brain cells, people "naturally" die within "the normal lifespan of 75 or 80 years."

But as I've already emphasized, due to the fact that Hayflick's Limit" was obtained by "culturing" brain cells in mind-*disconnected* glassware, it involves a process that, as we now know, is clearly invalid. Nevertheless, to verify his [strictly limited lifespan] theory, Hayflick tries to do so by saying this: "Nature planned things so that we would die *well before* we become old, and any efforts to extend life are really attempts to *fool* Mother Nature."

Although to overcome the "fooling nature by extending life" idea that "natural senescence" believers keep pushing, I say **HOORAY** for the people who, mainly by mind-over-body skills, become so adept at self-renewal, that they live **decades** beyond so-called "normal" life expectancy. For example, according to the world renown (for accuracy) Gerontology Research Group, since 1985, some 254 people have lived longer than 110 years. And the following is a list of the ten longest living members of that highly eminent group, these perpetually energized, praiseworthy people known as:

The Top Ten Super-Centenarians

(1). Jeanne Calment (of France), passed-on August 4, 1997, at the age of 122.

(2.) Sarah Knauss (of France) passed-on December 30, 1999, at the age of 119.

(3). Lucy Hannah (of the U.S), passed-on March 21, 1993, at the age of 117.

(4). Marie-Louise Meilleur (of Canada), passed-on August 29, 1998, at the age of 117.

(5). Maria Capovilla (of Ecuador), passed-on August 27, 2006, at the age of 116.

(6). Tane Ikai (of Japan), passed-on January 18, 1995, at the age of 116.

(7). Elizabeth Bolden (of the U.S.), passed-on December 11, 1995, at the age of 116.

(8). Carrie White (of the U.S.), passed-on February 14, 1991, at the age of 116.

(9). Komato Hongo (of Japan), passed-on October 31, 2003, at the age of 116.

(10). Maggie Barnes (of the U.S.) passed-on January 19, 1998, at the age of 115.

As the Gerontology Research Group list of 110-plus year-olds goes on and on, a list that documents the reality of people who, in life-preserving, conscientious ways, managed to learn the **ART** of ((**transcending**)) "normal" longevity—a quest that is **truly** universal.

Universal indeed, as by overcoming the depressing influences of [ageism], there arises the joyful possibility that, the longer we live, the more adept we get at initiating the ((inner-healing knowledge)) that keeps us perceptively alive and well.

However, a lot of self-empowering realizations comes from what I call the **Seeing Is Believing** dimension. And to help you **SEE** how the body reacts to what your brain first envisions, simply try out the following little test, whereby you can experience a small example of how ((mental-picturing)) can immediately effect the body.

Okay, to do this little (but actually very **BIG** when expanded) experiment, just close your eyes, and take a few seconds to imagine yourself throwing a baseball . . . .

If you did that, you probably felt your shoulders twitch (at the same time you pictured yourself throwing the ball), because when your mind visualizes your body doing something, there is always a physical reaction to that vision.

But to take the ((action-follows-thought)) phenomenon a giant-step further, let's look at how it works in regard to aging, as clarified by this quoted passage from Maxwell Maltz's aforementioned classic book—**Psycho-cybernetics**:

"I have no doubt that you could take a healthy man of 30 and within five years make an 'old man' of him, if you could somehow convince him to picture himself as being very old, and that all physical activity was dangerous, and that mental activity was futile. Also, if you could induce him to give up his dreams for the future, give up all interest in new ideas, to regard himself as 'washed up' and 'worthless,' I am sure that you could experimentally create an old man."

But what Dr. Maltz describes as just an experiment is, all too often, what happens via the "normal" conception of "aging" throughout this planet.

And yet I'm here to cultivate a vastly **different** plan—a view of the future that goes far beyond the basic "normality" that, mainly due to a lack of education, makes us turn away from the ultimate, ((truly conscious)) duty of saving one's precious body.

And as I described earlier, a classic example of that struggle was John Huston, a man who, after his trio of doctors predicted that he had only "a few months" to live, instead of falling for their [Old Era] perceptions, he arose into four more years of a vibrantly significant life.

But again I ask **WHY** is it so accepted for physicians to tell us **WHEN** we are expected to die? Can these inappropriate forecasts be mentally depressing enough to **worsen** a disease? So toss those [negative-thought-waves/death predicting-"practices"] **AWAY** I say, because if giving us mind and body expiration dates is "good medicine," then surely I'm on the wrong planet at the wrong time.

But as for the results of my Massage and Talk sessions, quite unlike the coldly separated, [doctor deals-with-customer's-body] process, by connecting with the mind of who I work on, instead of a "patient" who just silently lays there, I get memorable feedback, such as when John Huston told me this:

"Well Jesse, I've spent a fortune on these . . . supposedly medical experts who, for over a year now, have been filling me with lots of drugs. But even after going through all of that, now they say that my emphysema is . . . apparently beyond being cured. Yeah, well, at this point, it feels like I've been talked into dying and being robbed at the same time. And what could be more debilitating than that?"

And surely that's a far too common feeling, a dilemma linked to the brain suppressing, profit-based idea that "standard" medical procedures should, quite inflexibly, disregard self-curing, mental abilities, and only focus on a patient's (apparently visible), physical condition.

But to advance onto effectively metaphysical methods of healthcare, I offer this book as a true-to-life, genuinely progressive outcome of four decades of worldwide research. And by traversing this global journey, you can learn the (body-saving) secrets of Vietnamese Buddhists, along with the vitally therapeutic wisdom of an amazingly ageless, 121 year-old, Tunisian mystic, followed by a visit with a truly enlightening, Ecuadorian Incan healer who, at 118, looks like 55 or 60.

But before we further our exploration into the awareness-expanding, steadily beneficial realm of ((ongoing regeneration)), I will sum-up this chapter with another of my (hopefully) uplifting song-poems—the one that I've come to call—

From This Point On—

Mind-activated-healing will be **truly unfurled**—
to spread its vast benefits **throughout the WORLD**—
Teaching us to ((**revive**)) the **full POTENCY** of our **brains**—
whereby we **TRANSCEND** ills and "aging" and pains—
As ((**self-curing**)) knowledge will no longer be [hidden]—
by [Old Era] greed that wants to keep it [forbidden]—
But with liberated minds we ((**focus**)) **on PREVENTION**—
arousing ((**protective**)) ways that need **more attention**—
helping us to ((emanate)) **SELF-DIRECTED defenses**—
amid which we maintain **all EIGHT of our senses**—
As it's ((**NEW ERA TIME**)) **for the ((UNIVERSAL)) mind**—
that leaves [Tube-View] thinking light-years **behind**—
As brain and body learn to ((**vitally UNIFY**))—
to **STRENGTHEN** restoration, **not** letting it *die*—
So sit back and relax, and **ENJOY** this **brain-food**—
to nourish ((**empowerment**)) that's long been [*subdued*]—
Yes, read on dear reader, read **ON** and you will **SEE**—
Truly **WORKING** ways to ((**ENLIGHTEN**)) **your destiny** . . .

(((CHAPTER TWO)))

TRULY EFFECTIVE METHODS
OF ((HEALING-SELF-RENEWAL))
REVEALED

"If you are not willing to learn, no one can help you. But
if you are determined to learn, no one can stop you."
— Thomas Edison

"The whole secret of salvation hinges on the conversion of
word to deed, with and through the whole being."
— Henry Miller

Thus it's "with and through our whole being" that ((healing
knowledge)) can save us from disease and physical decay,
whereby the human body's amazing array of abilities keep
steadily functioning, perpetually re-created by an ((internal
universe)) of self-renewing energy.

But due to the fact that ongoing regeneration involves the
very complicated activities of various organs, surely humanity
can be greatly helped by a well researched, body-maintenance
instruction manual.

Therefore, to fulfill a vital part of that need, this chapter
traverses what I call **The New Era of Mind-Over-Body
Tour**—a crucially informative journey that begins by pointing
out the important differences between:

Voluntary and Involuntary Muscles

Due to the fact that physical durability greatly depends on what happens either **automatically** or **voluntarily** (within us), we begin this literary tour of your body's phenomenal amount of duties by focusing on what are called:

Involuntary Muscles: These are the parts of your body that are consistently spontaneous, the muscle groups called "visceral" and/or "cardiac" muscles, those which operate vital organs such as the heart, liver, kidneys and intestines. All of which are controlled by what is called the "autonomic" nervous system (which is an anatomy textbook way of saying automatic). But the most useful focus of our word-to-deed conversion right now is to (woo-ha!) **consciously** direct, the ever-at-your-service:

Voluntary Muscles: Also called "striated" or "skeletal muscle," these are the body parts controlled by what is called the "somatic" nervous system—a neural network that voluntarily directs the function of the following, regularly exercised muscles: the face, neck, arms, hands, legs and feet muscles, along with the abdominal muscles, plus the chest and back muscles. And although you may not realize it, your **skin** is also part of the somatic muscle system, and is thereby a **voluntarily** controlled organ. But that control largely depends on relatively unexplored, intentionally ((mind-directed)) methods, effective techniques such the **You-nity Sessions** (clearly described later in this chapter).

However, for now, let's move on with our **Mind-Over-Body Tour** by taking another look at the ((central-brain-emanations)) that make the whole interconnection of mind-to-body happen. And to get a brief glimpse of that vital phenomenon, I will again ask you to close your eyes for a half-minute, just to have another insightful view of the ((creational energy)) inside you . . .

Okay then, if you took that brief exploration into your ((inner world/metaphysical body)), surely you saw the tiny particles of light shimmering within the darkness, because even a blind person (which you're obviously not) can see those ceaselessly glittering flashes within. As we are again re-minded that there is no total darkness in this world, but the continually luminous display of the ((regenerative forces)) that heals and energizes every living being.

All of which is a ((thought-wave-echoing)) process much like what enables TV sets to re-create sound and images via the ((energy-impulses) sent via an antenna, cable or satellite dish. But instead of reproducing sound and images that are electronically re-created by a television, your ((central-brain-regenerator)) processes thought-waves that initiate all of your mental and physical, self-renewing functions.

But despite the vast potentials of learning how to mentally-direct the healing powers within us, even in these so-called "modern" times, this vitally progressive approach is still seen as somewhat "far-fetched"—an attitude that calls to mind this famous quote from Albert Einstein:

> **"Our knowledge about mankind is still in its infancy."**

But dear Mr. Einstein, if you were still alive, I would love to ask you this continually significant question:

If the perpetually restorative energy (of which I write and speak), truly **IS** the inborn power that activates physical regeneration, why hasn't the "scientific community" taken the time to give this vitally important "stuff" a **NAME**? Are self-directed curing abilities really *that* unthinkable?

But after nearly forty years of being unable to find an official title for this yet-to-be-labeled, force-of-life "whatever," I've gone ahead and given it a handle that we are getting well acquainted with: **Creational Energy (C.E.).**

Thus in regard to the principal ((central-brain)) generator of **C.E.**, our **New Era of Mind-Over-Body Tour** now duly focuses on—

The Phenomenally Potent Pineal Gland

After two decades of studying the workings of this unparalleled organ, I have come to see it as **The Initial Spark of Human Physicality**, mainly because of this significant fact:

The pineal is located in the exact **CENTER** of the human brain's healing and rejuvenation system, and when a newborn baby is created in the womb, **the FIRST body-part that is formed is the pineal.**

But despite that unique distinction, [Old Era] medical science continually disregards the vital duties of the pineal gland, mainly because their methods only deal with physical substances, while the central function of the pineal is to emanate ((**energy**)). And so for the most part, the phenomenal pineal remains a vastly unexplored, "mysterious" organ.

However, to counteract the lack of public attention given to this extremely influential part of the human brain, I will now provide some well-researched, cutting-edge information about the basic purposes of what I call:

The Mighty Master Gland:

(1). The pineal strongly protects the human body against what is called "neural-degeneration," a function which, in plain English, means that this organ perpetually emanates ((restorative energy)) to **every** part of the human body.

(2). The pineal gland steadily circulates MCH (Melanin Concentrating Hormone), a secretion that protects us against melanoma skin cancers, while it also greatly alleviates pain, mainly by activating a very potent, internal (pain-blocker) called "endorphins."

(3). The pineal helps to keep our immunity systems thoroughly working during the body's nighttime slumber, strongly protecting us from diseases by initiating the ((subconsciously healing powers)) of the (central-brain) area.

All of which are crucial duties that make the pineal what could be called: **The Principal Generator of the Human Body's Healing-Energy**

Thus by utilizing my studies into the vast abilities of the pineal's ((body-saving emanations)), I have developed an effectively rejuvenating method of ((mentally directed)). self-healing massage. And if you want to try this easily done technique on yourself, I will now describe how it's activated—this the regeneration-reviving process that I call:

The You-nity Session

First of all, the most therapeutic way to begin a You-nity Session, is to focus on an area (at the back of your neck) that can be heard, felt and found simply by leaning your head back, or tilting it from side to side. And to hear and feel what I'm talking about, just nod your head forward and back, or gently roll it in a circle . . .

If you did that simple process, I'm sure that you heard a small crackling-sound that comes from a wad of pain and tension (located above the top of your spine). And what that glob of neck pain is, dear reader, is an area that I call the **Ex-tensioning Spot** (or the **X-Spot**)—the place that biology books call the "medulla oblongata" region, the "tree-trunk" of the brain, from which pineal-radiated neurons steadily flow. Through this single location, all of the brain's healing commands travel in and out of the medulla oblongata (gateway) from the brain—through-the-body—and then back again. But whatever you call that highly significant spot doesn't really matter, just so you don't forget to keep it unclogged, as any blockage there inhibits mind-power prevention of physical decay (much like having a leak in your brain-to-body-**unity**, fuel line).

And so we begin a (skin-healing) You-nity Session by de-tensioning the X-Spot area at the back of your neck, a treatment that is especially needed if you're like me, spending several hours a day stiffening up while working the keys of a computer.

But to capably clear and loosen up the medulla/X-Spot area, it's easily done by raking away its (stored up) tension with a press-and-release, kneading motion, done with your fingers. Yes, just press and release, press and release—surely a relaxing, feel-good procedure, especially soothing if you keep in mind this delightfully ((self-empowering)) fact:

The future of your body is in good hands—**YOURS**.

Alright then, with that uplifting thought in mind, we will now move on to the next step of the You-nity Session, whereby we can activate the spine-tingling sensation of—

Energy-Connecting the Body's Power-Points

This vitality-reviving process is simply done by rubbing a small, softly massaged circle at the center of your forehead, while also using your other hand to loosen up the X-Spot—thereby de-tensioning your forebrain and medulla regions at the same time. And for an extra buzz while you do this, close your eyes and envision a sparkling stream of C.E. passing from your (forehead-rubbing) fingertips—flowing on through the **pineal** and X-Spot and then down through the rest of your body—Va-woom!—this is **truly** a refreshing, stress-relieving procedure.

However, don't just take my word for it, go ahead and give this X-Spot/ pineal/medulla-connection a try, and you will see how it truly alleviates tension-caused "aging" from your face . . .

But that therapeutic procedure is just the beginning of a You-nity Session, because next comes the ((mind-powered)) facial massage part of it, a genuinely effective technique which I will now explain.

To initiate this process, close your eyes and again do a (circular motion) forehead rub, but this time notice how a ball of sparkling of light appears where you are massaging it into activation—a cluster of radiating energy that I have come to call the ((**Internal Sun**)).

Then, after seeing the formation of ((healing light)) brighten and expand where you do a circular rub, try the same process on one side of your brow, and then on the other side, and watch how these glittering emanations gather at the same place that you are massaging . . .

What causes these delightful ((clusters)) of creational energy to be directed, is the combined power of (**focus and touch),** whereby you create the same (self-repairing/connection) that happens via the natural urge to relieve pain by ((rubbing)) it away. But by purposely **stimulating** and **SEEING** healing evocations in action, you thereby **maximize** the power of your ((self-mending)) skills—doing so by emanating a process that is both physical and metaphysical at the same time.

Okay then, after activating that ((healing-energy-expanding)) procedure, the next step of the You-nity Session is use your **C.E.**-charged fingers to do the facial revitalizing part of it—a method that **truly** diminishes what has come to be called "wrinkles."

Wrinkles, shrinkles, and why are alive (and thereby **changeable**), energy-controlled things labeled a noun? But to revise our perception of those so-called "wrinkles," we can give them some ((verbal energy)) by calling them wrinkling, because with a new name, they take on a newly clarified identity, and thereby become much more **controllable**. And it's amid an increased comprehension of body-control, that this de-wrinkling process is perpetually actualized, especially while realizing this crucial fact:

Beneath every "wrinkle" there is a wad of pain (an ache quickly felt when you rub a facial indentation). And that small (pocket of pain) is THE factor which CAUSES a (muscle-tension) "wrinkle" to happen. Therefore, truly effective de-wrinkling is mainly activated by one vital process: massaging away the pain (beneath EVERY "wrinkle").

Thus newly-empowered by knowing **WHY** so-called "wrinkles" appear, if you have any unwanted (pain-lines) on your forehead, that's a good place to begin testing the effects of what I call an Energy-Makeup/You-nity session.

A truly capable way to diminish forehead lines, is to pull the skin there **upward** towards your hairline, using a repeated, finger-raking motion. But to optimize this procedure, close your eyes to **see** the **C.E.** do its ((healing-energy-sparking)) thing, all while you massage the lines (**temporarily**) etched into the (**voluntary**) muscles under your skin. Yes, sweeping **AWAY** (muscle-tension-caused) "wrinkles"—a practice greatly helped by visualizing those (pockets of pain) going directly to the **center** of you mind (where all painful discomfort is duly relieved by pineal-secreted endorphins).

Then, while staying aware of the **alive and changeable** nature of "wrinkles," if you have any (eye area) "crow's feet," you can quickly diminish those indentations by softly finger-raking and ((**RELEASING**)) them via the C.E.-stimulated power of your ((**healing touch**)).

And following that, by utilizing the same (tension and pain-removing massage), you can capably minimize the "jowls" that tend to form along each side of your nose.

But to make this (willpower-strengthening) process continuously rejuvenating, it needs to be done **DAILY,** all while being reminded of this steadily useful fact:

When you tell your body to walk, it walks, and when you tell it to write something—**HELLO**—it gets written, because your body is **SUPPOSED** to follow your instructions, true? So then why shouldn't you at least **TRY** the You-nity/Skin-Renewal process, just to see if you can **MAKE** it work?

However, the most effective way to firm-up and resuscitate skin, is to massage your face and body with fingers that are kept wet with water, thereby doing what I call **Water Activation Massage (WAM)**—a technique that deepens the penetration of what is truly—

The Ultimate Liquid

Due to the fact that skin and tissue is 70 percent water, we can potently reinforce a You-nity Session by utilizing **C.E.** combined with the only **TRULY** moisturizing and de-wrinkling substance—plain **water.**

Although I do realize that a lot of you women out there regularly use make-up, so you may be reluctant to do Water Activation Massage as often as I utilize it (which is two or three times a day, with each ((facial-rehydration)) session lasting about one minute). But even though it may necessitate reapplying make-up, I'm sure that by (**seeing**) the face-renewing results of ((Ultimate Liquid-penetrating)), WAM sessions, you will delightfully discover that it is well worth taking the time to do it.

Also, it helps to realize that the key element of the Water Activation Massage is the fact that, by merging water with ((intently focused)) creational energy, every massaged skin "cell" quickly binds with the hundreds of water molecules (that surround and regenerate it). All of which is a process that begins with being **born** in a (womb) filled with body-creating, life-sustaining water—a truism that points to this significant reality:

Nothing on Earth can replace the life-originating, flesh-revitalizing properties of water.

Therefore, despite the constant barrage of ads about so-called "skin moisturizers," **ALL** of these products are [**more dense**] than water, and are thereby **unable** to penetrate into (**water-based**) skin. And this is easily proven by the fact that lotions or creams will **always** float to the surface of water, totally unable to merge with it.

And with that truism firmly realized, yet another beneficial aspect of the WAM session, is its ability to be done almost anywhere, simply by going to a sink where, with a bottle of purified water, you can enjoy a refreshing ((and truly absorbing)), facial massage. And while vitally rehydrating your face, you are also **safely** cleaning it, mainly by avoiding the skin-drying (and pore-clogging) effects of soap (or so-called "skin cleansers.")

Hang On to Your Hat

Also note that, when at the beach, or any place that steadily exposures you to direct sunlight, instead of damaging your skin with the harsh chemicals of "sun-block," simply wear a wide-brimmed hat, a safe and effective way to avoid the face-wrinkling effects of sunrays. And be sure to bring a bottle of water along, both for rubbing it on your skin (to keep intense heat from drying it out), and of course drinking it to keep yourself rehydrated.

Alright then, let's now move on to the next step of the You-nity Session, where I uncover a truly rejuvenating process that, quite surprisingly, has yet to be widely discovered and utilized, a simple technique that reveals how to:

Self-Renew and Tighten-Up the Neck Area

Have you ever noticed that when softly pulling on tiny patches of neck skin with your fingers, little particles of it can be easily peeled off? This is because the top layer of skin is what dermatologists call the "dead layer"—while underneath that are the "living layers" of skin.

And as to why the "dead layer" is especially removable in the neck area, it's because there is a large amount of sweat glands there that continually loosen-up, ready-to-be-shed skin.

Therefore, by noticing how dust-like pieces of neck skin can be peeled off, bit by tiny bit, we are again reminded that **ALL** bodily skin is ceaselessly replacing itself, so much so, that research reveals this amazing (but scientifically verified) fact:

Nearly 50-percent of house dust comes from naturally discarded skin!

Yes, that **IS** amazing, but quite true. And due to the continuous reality of dead-skin shedding (especially prevalent in the sweat-glands-loaded, neck area), you can, quite easily, perpetuate renewal of that part of your body, simply by doing the following procedure:

A (finger-raking) massage that, piece by tiny piece, can peel away particles of ready-to-be-shed, neck skin, a genuinely effective, neck-re-toning method that I do several times a day, merely by taking a minute to utilize this very simple, (((dead-skin-removing))) technique.

Then, to further refurbish the neck area, after doing the neck-peeling process, to keep the skin there from hanging loosely (due to unexercised, lacking-in-firmness, neck muscles), a simple way to re-strengthen the coil of tendons there is this:

A few times a day, place your hand (or both hands) on top of your head, and then apply a firmly downward pressure, while at the same time you counter-pressure your hand(s) with your neck muscles, doing this while you tilt your head from side-to-side, or roll it in a circle.

Further yet, try to keep in mind that, by utilizing the You-nity Session methods of skin renewal, these techniques also help to arouse ((healing energy circulation))—doing so by loosening-up (and thereby de-clogging) the flow of **C.E.** through your (back-of-neck) **X-Spot**.

Okay then, following those skin revitalizing procedures, let's move on to the final segment of the daily You-nity Session, whereby we focus on a ((creational energy-igniting)) way to:

Take Control of C.E.-Depleted "Graying" and Hair-Fall

First of all, I should duly emphasize that hair is an extension of the cerebrum-controlled part of the brain (as are the cerebral senses of vision and touch). And it's the (touch-sensitive) properties of hair follicles that has brought me to discover the truly potent, ((follicle-re-energizing)) effects of regularly massaging one's entire scalp.

Therefore, by giving yourself a daily ((hair-roots-reviving)), fingertip rub, not only are you helping to restore the naturally inborn color of your hair, you are also stimulating your ability to keep it healthy and steadily growing.

However, mainly because of Big Pharma's massively advertised, supposedly "hair-growing" potions, the fact that baldness can be avoided by self-massage has, quite unfortunately, remained continually overlooked.

But anyway, despite being steadily suppressed by ads that vastly exaggerate the curative results of pharmaceutical concoctions, by thinking "outside of the [box]," truly effective, cost-free methods will take their justified, genuinely earned place in the realms of physical repair.

Alright then, now that my perpetually beneficial, You-nity Session techniques have been clearly made known, let us now move onto the next part of our **New Era of Mind-Over-Body**

Tour, whereby we focus on a factor of self-renewal based on the vital process of:

Quelling [Body-Damaging] Anger

More and more I realize that one's physical appearance, for the most part, is a perception-based vision—a mental projection that can quickly shift from one (situations-influenced) look to another, depending on what thoughts are entering our minds.

Thus by realizing the powerful effects of what we focus on, [inner-resentment] can, quite effectively, be quelled by limiting our exposure to news broadcasts about death and destruction, all of which involve very saddening, basically useless information.

But of course, the process of transcending [gloom-and-doom] programming is much more complex than minimizing one's intake of bad news, especially in light of this significant fact:

"Global studies reveal that the most illness-producing factor is steadily ongoing anger, an extremely health-endangering attitude that, for various reasons, is habitually disregarded as being merely a so-called hot temper."

Therefore, to justifiably subdue emotional explosions, keep in mind that they are ((blood-pressure-raising)) reactions, whereby you vastly increase your chances of inducing a heart attack or stroke.

For just as the great Buddha said: "Holding onto anger is like drinking poison, and then expecting it to do no damage to your body."

And yet even if it makes you feel somewhat "weak" to let go of resentment, according to worldwide research, by duly releasing [long-held grudges], the likelihood of enjoying a healthy and happy, productive life is greatly enlarged.

Although mostly due to so-called "cultural" influences, developing a pleasantly positive attitude is widely seen as "unmanly," a belief that, to a large extent, stems from the perception that men are the "traditionally" grim, "nose-to-the-grindstone" providers.

All of which has fostered the concept that, by being the customary protector of the family, men should be steadily serious and rarely amused, because a blissful attitude supposedly weakens what is regarded as "manly toughness." And maybe that is why male homosexuals are commonly called "gays," because obvious gayety is not an attitude that "real men" should display. Okay then, I guess that makes me an "unmanly," joyfully happily heterosexual—a cheerful fellow who plans to **stay** that way.

Yes indeed, and as to the belief in the healthful "superiority" of "manly toughness," according to international statistics, the average lifespan of women is several years longer than what it is for men, mainly because women tend to pay much closer attention to their bodies.

Nevertheless, regardless of one's gender, to transcend the notion that, as we age, we get increasingly "over the hill," I believe that getting over so-called "hills" helps us to build up momentum, whereby we can overcome one physical test "hill" after another. And also, via "leaps of faith," we learn to grow wings that, on the way down, can ((joyfully)) uplift us.

All of which is a process that has me frequently analyzing my perception of what enjoyment is, and at this so-called "senior citizen" phase of my life, I find that most of my beneficial pleasure comes from the learning process, a relatively ((infinite)) dimension of awareness that I call:

((Self-Designed Time))

The main objective of this mode of thinking is, quite essentially, taking the time to meditate on this truly prominent fact: what we (whisper) to ourselves is, in the long run, far more therapeutic that what we say out loud.

But on the [[furiously hollering]], angry side of the fence, more and more I see reports about the effects of hate-mongering violence, an attitude that is a major cause of homicides, especially among city-dwelling teenagers.

In fact, largely due to the supposedly "New Youth Culture" called "hip-hop" music, there's been a massive upsurge of "drive-by-shootings," whereby "gangster-rappers" have popularized the "action movie" gunplay that, quite obviously, has been programmed into their minds.

But being the reggae music, peace and harmony-style singer that I am, even though the "hip-hop gangsta" scene may be hugely profitable for its promoters, I see it as an overly vicious, tune-lacking form of "entertainment."

Although recently, on [TV], I saw a "hip-hop" band that, instead of molesting my melody-loving ears, had me chuckling at their lyrics, especially when the female "rapper" of the group, to my shocked surprise, shouted at the leader of the band, telling him this:

"**Hey** bro, stop treating me like a street-corner **ho!** And also brush your teeth, because your breath is **smelly,** and try to do something about your bulging **beer-belly!**"

Oh gosh yes, those were some zany lyrics that really me got me laughing. And then she followed that boldly comical, get-your-act-together line with this, somewhat comforting one:

"And instead of always acting like a **thug,** just come over here and **give** me a big **hug!**"

Yes indeed, a little bit of humor and ((heart-twanging)) warmth is surely what the "hip-hop," so-called "culture" needs, and thereby that overly macho, anger-sparked arena will become more conscious of their words, actions and offensive tones of voice.

But probably the worst thing about the rap-music, "ruff-house-dancehall" scene, is the way it pulls teenagers into the [[double-whammy]] of body-damaging tobacco and booze, a situation that, in the long run, can gradually transform them into what is satirized by the following anecdote:

Two bald-headed, very sad looking, elderly men sit at a barroom booth, drearily staring at two dozen empty beer bottles (scattered on the table in front of them). And after putting out his cigar in a butt-filled ashtray, one of the men says:

"Hey Charlie, do you see those two sickly looking, very old drunks over there? That's **US** in ten years."

And then the other one says this:

"**Duh**! You're so constantly plastered that you don't even realize it, but that's **OUR** reflection in the **mirror**!"

And indeed that is a satire both funny and sad. First of all, on the sad side, the more steadily addicted people become to alcohol, the more difficult it is to recognize themselves in a mirror, whereby they increasingly become strangers to [themselves].

But on the funny side of that situation, there's the widespread belief that being a "champion" booze-guzzler is, according to beer commercials, a way to make grumpy people "happily stronger," whereby a six-pack of brew can make them more like the "**REAL** men" in the ads.

And as to the so-called "manly" habit of producing an increasingly burgeoning "beer-belly," I recently read a rather funny joke about that [health-endangering] notion—a true-to-life gag that says this:

"If a man loses ten pounds off his ((bulgingly protruding)) stomach, his penis grows another inch. Why?

Because he can then **see** it!"

And with that said (and perhaps laughed at), let's move on to another of the sometimes humorous, but mainly ((self-healing)) themes of this book, this one being a process that I've found to be amazingly therapeutic—a nightly procedure that I call:

Inner-Directions

Surely this is an exciting part of this book for me, because it describes a self-curing technique that has become a centerpiece of my teachings—an effectively life-improving concept that I've been successfully utilizing for over two decades.

And as to what initially inspired me to develop the Inner Directions (I.D.) dimension of self-curing, it all began with this unforgettable realization:

For some continually mysterious reason, the normally conscious human brain uses about 10 percent of its curative powers, while the (subconscious) part utilizes the remaining 90 percent.

Thus in regard to why our extrasensory abilities remain a vastly unexplored, "mysterious" ability, I again emphasize that it's mainly because strictly [three-dimensional] research habitually ignores the ((fourth-dimension activated)), metaphysical realm of our minds.

But to advance beyond the [Old Era], material level perceptions of our regenerative abilities, Inner Directions sessions motivate the ((healing energy emanating)), pineal region, where the human body's (self-repairing and immunity systems) are initially activated.

However, mainly because intentionally stimulated, curative powers are such a relatively overlooked phenomenon, in order to capably utilize this vital capacity of the human brain, a certain amount of mental preparation is needed.

First of all, it's important to realize that much like what is called "self-hypnosis," the Inner Directions process is most potently initiated during a (calmly relaxed frame of mind), such as when you're ready for your nightly sleep. And then later, during the (slumbering creativity) zone of what I call **Rebirth Dreamtime**, your pre-sleep (inner-voiced) directions will evoke their penetrating effects. But to clearly grasp the reasoning involved with this method, it may be helpful to ask yourself the following two questions:

Question 1 (Regarding the Hidden-Universe of Dreams):

Have you ever wondered why we so often hear about "making dreams come true," despite the fact that, almost everything visualized while we sleep is either easily forgotten, or it conveys a message that has no clearly helpful purpose?

Question 2 (Regarding the Hidden-Universe of Dreams):

Due to the fact that we spend nearly one-third of our lives sleeping, other than just rest and relaxation, are there important benefits hidden amid the (subconscious) dimension that are yet to be widely understood, and thereby utilized for our personal well being?

Therefore, in order to tap-into the vastly disregarded, 90 percent of the human brain's ((subconsciously-self-curing)) abilities, I have thoroughly developed the truly effective, cost-free technique that I call Inner Directions.

And if you would like to explore the many benefits of this uniquely beneficial procedure, tonight perhaps, when you're ready for your nightly slumber, you can initiate this invaluable process by doing the following, (inner-voiced) preparation:

The first step of an Inner Directions (I.D.) session is to decide on some sincerely wanted, physical changes that you would like to see happen to your body (such as stimulating the repair of an ailment, or whatever self-renewing healings come to mind).

For example, the following (I.D. invoked) message is one that I've been continually working for many years, a somewhat (all-inclusive), songlike invocation that says basically this:

Dear body-god of my healing energy, please keep me disease-free, pain-free, tension-free, worry-free and

wrinkles-free, steadily helping me to regenerate myself perpetually . . .

But of course, you can formulate you own list of personal desires, as we all tend to have a large variety of physical and mental needs.

However, before you (inner-voice) your self-curing directions, to strengthen the power of their penetration, it greatly helps to clear your mind of any thoughts that might distract you from whatever you want your I.D. messages to accomplish. And via my multitude of experimentation with this process, I have found that a very effective way to de-clutter the pathway for successfully achieved invocations is this:

((Mentally repeat)) these three words several times: **Clear, sleep, heal.**

And then, after several recitations of **clear, sleep, heal**, it greatly helps their activation by visualizing the following, (willpower-strengthening) dimension of thought:

Deeply perceive your mind as a generator of strongly ((healing-energy)), thereby sparking the ((mind's-body-teamwork)) that makes dreams work, because (brainpower flows where attention goes), and realizing that is a vital part of the I.D. process. All while keeping in mind that a **central key** to making these sessions truly activated is this momentous fact:

Although we can't always influence what goes on outside us, we can **LEARN** to effectively initiate what happens ((**INSIDE**)) us.

Alright then, with that ((self-empowering)) proclamation in mind, along with pre-sleep instructions, let us now focus on another (Rebirth Dreamtime) procedure that you can add to your Inner Directions list of desires, a truly rejuvenating technique that I call:

Photo Self-Imaging

To enable this method of deeply stimulating ((mind-over-body regeneration)), the first step is to look though the collection of photos of yourself, and then choose one that reveals an especially youthful look—perhaps a picture from several years ago.

Then, just before you go to sleep, (intensely focus) on that snapshot (for at least a minute), thoroughly concentrating on it so that, even with your eyes closed, you can vividly recall its image. And after doing that, the next step is to initiate an Inner Directions message that says basically this:

"Dear precious body-god, I believe that our self-renewing system is now working better than ever. And so by tomorrow morning, I want to see myself looking more like that picture, as by merging mind and body together as one unit, surely our healing energy can **MAKE** that process happen."

Thus by regularly evoking that instruction, it's become an I.D. procedure that I have found to be amazingly transformative, and if done with a ((**persistent**)) belief in your ((regenerative)) abilities, it should work for **you too**. And as to why I'm so certain about that, after writing about Inner Directions techniques in my Awareness magazine column, I was soon deluged with a multitude of thankful emails, all of which confirmed the truly positive effects of pre-sleep, ((dream-designing)) sessions.

Although I should mention the fact that, to get steadily beneficial results from the I.D. method of mind-over-body self-renewal, it largely depends on being mentally strong enough to transcend the following, so-called "medical establishment" belief:

"Results gained by merely metaphysical means are usually undependable, because they deny all of the laws of physical chemistry, and are thereby *unscientific* results."

However, **results are results**, and what gets the job done can ((**continue**)) to get it done, because a method that works **once** can work **thousands** of times, even if it's not yet an "officially instituted" science.

And as to the so-called "physical chemistry" of I.D. sessions on my face, every time that I forget to do my nightly, pre-sleep invocations, by the following morning, I can clearly see that (previously erased) "wrinkles" are again reappearing. As I repeatedly find that regeneration-sparking, continual self-renewal mainly depends on developing a steadily maintained amount of one truly indispensable factor: ((**DETERMINATION**)). All while realizing that directing ((kind thoughts)) to one's body creates a (truly **penetrating**) energy.

And even if Plan A of your Inner Directions doesn't always work, just try another plan, because the metaphysical alphabet has 25 more, ((ready-to-be-activated)) letters.

For example, I have found that Plan S of the I.D. process is to alleviate sleeplessness, the so-called "insomnia" that often comes with "aging." And if you ever encounter a sustained inability to get enough slumber time, there's a (central-brain-emanating) technique that works far quicker (and safer) than sleeping pills, mainly by doing the following invocation:

While laying in bed and trying to go to sleep, (inner voice) a FIRMLY commanding, chant-like instruction that says basically this:

I am TOTALLY in control of my precious mind, body and soul, and right now I'm directing myself to sleep-now . . . sleep-now . . . sleep-now . . .

But while doing this simple (but strongly penetrating) recitation, it helps to keep in mind that a good night's sleep is **crucial** to one's health and safety, especially if chronic drowsiness has a tendency to make people bleary-eyed while driving a vehicle.

Also, along with the (sleeplessness avoiding), Inner Directions Plan S, I have developed what I call:

Inner Directions Plan R

With due persistence, this is the I.D. invocation that effectively remedied my rheumatism (the painful malady also known as "arthritis"). As despite the pharmaceutical claims that this ailment is "incurable," it took only three pre-sleep, ((dream-directing)) sessions to heal the arthritic pain that I had in my hands. And surely this is no small victory, considering reports that say that, worldwide, arthritis now has over 300 million people taking pain-relieving pills to alleviate this increasingly widespread affliction.

But due to the fact that this muscle-aching malfunction was originally called "rheumatism," I was spurred to wonder why "Big Pharma" changed its name to "arthritis." Could it be that chemical corporations converged on the notion that, in order to increase the profits made by selling pain-numbing pills for rheumatism, to make this ailment sound more "right" for us, they decided to call it "arthritis?" Therefore, well aware of the ((perception power)) of what something is named, to overcome the supposedly "right-for-us" disease called "arthritis," I tried some I.D. evocations that perceived it as being what I now call it arth**WRONG**us. And lo and behold, after three sessions of calling it that, it's been many months since "arthritis" has [**wrongly**] ached my hands.

As I again realize that, more than anything else, perceptions ((**rule**)) our regenerative abilities, from the first day of physical life until the day when our ((healing-soul-power)) decides to give up its body, and thereby reincarnate into a new one. And on and on it goes like that, ever-self-renewing and (hopefully) **learning** . . .

Thus with the perpetual abilities of ((undying resolve)) steadily kept in mind, I will now wrap-up the Inner Directions part of this book by recalling my most extremely difficult test of the I.D. process, back when I had what is called a "near-death experience."

As our **New Era of Mind-Over-Body Tour** now journeys across this beautiful planet to the lushly tropical country of Vietnam, whereby I can share some (perhaps life-saving) insights acquired during what I call:

My Ultimate Inner Directions Test: Saved by Re-entering My Body

Oh memory, memory, if I **totally** lose you, how can I remember what is **true**? Yes indeed, memory is very important for our survival, because without the ability of recalling lessons that we've learned, any form of education would be totally useless.

Thus I feel very fortunate to have what is called "photographic recall," and due to that capacity, the incident that I will now describe is not, in any way, fictionalized or imagined, but is steadily based on true-to-life, unexaggerated reality (as is **ALL** of this book).

And with that duly emphasized, I will now (quite accurately) transcribe this rather traumatic, unforgettable experience.

Rewinding now, deep into my memory banks, revisiting the year of 1965, back to when young men were getting drafted into the U.S. army. And because I was amid a one-year leave of absence from college, in May of that year, shortly after turning 21, I became eligible for the "Uncle Sam needs YOU," so-called "crucial duty" of being a soldier in the Vietnam War.

Anyway, dreadfully (long-story-short), in November of 1966, while doing what my infantry squad called "jungle ambush patrol," I had a seizure-like, coma-producing, malaria attack, whereby I was soon in a helicopter, being swiftly taken to a military field hospital.

Then, after a week of being bedded-down in a very dreary, tent-covered malaria ward (during which I saw a dozen young soldiers die from that terrible disease), I was told that I had the same "very lethal, malarial strain" that killed those twelve men.

Therefore, because I had what they said was an 'incurable"
illness, I immersed myself into a totally focused, day and night
effort to evoke what I now call Inner Directions sessions, amid
which I realized that self-initiated willpower might be my only
way to survive.

However, at that time, after being deeply inspired by a
Buddhist priest who, just a few days before I was taken to
that hospital, I had a long conversation with, most of my
inner-voiced, (hopefully) curative evocations went something
like this:

"Come **on** now, Jesse, **wake up** your healing powers,
because I **KNOW** that we can beat this disease, Because just as
that Buddhist priest said, to overcome **any** illness, we need to
tap-into the ((Spiritual Body Within)). Yes, that's **IT,** the healing
force that activates the very **center** of our minds, where **all** cures
begin their life-saving effects.

As on and on my I.D. sessions went like that, hoping to
merge with the part of my brain that could save me, despite
the fact that a month of malaria had made me a pathetic bag of
bones, too weak to even stand up.

And it was amid that emaciated, barely alive state of being
that a nurse told me basically this:

"Well son, now that your temperature is running so lethally
high, plus the blood tests that say your body-decaying, parasite
rate is beyond control, I can see that it's time to call in . . .
captain Murphy, the military pastor who, quite kindly, gives his
blessings to the near-death patients here. So then, if it's okay
to you, I will have him come to your bedside, so that he can
help to guide you through your passing into . . . the heavenly
afterlife."

"Oh really? But nurse Julie, maybe you don't realize the
strength I have **inside,**" I recall saying to her, very reluctant
to believe that all hope for my survival was gone. And then I
told her about what that English speaking, Buddhist priest said
about metaphysical-level, self-curing. "Have you heard about
the disease defeating, spiritual ways of that these people teach in

their temples?" I asked her, suddenly feeling strong enough to sit up and face her directly.

"No . . . I don't believe that I have," she said. "But do whatever method of . . . hopeful prayer that you can, and may God bless you for your efforts."

And then, later that night, I experienced a vividly memorable occurrence, one that seemed like a dream, but it was a true-to-life slice of reality. As suddenly I saw myself ((rising above)) the material world whereby, somehow, I could see my (lifeless corpse?) in the bed beneath me—a truly stunning transformation that bought to mind the following question:

Did that Buddhist priest speak the truth when he told me that, by transcending the physical body and becoming "pure-spirit," we thereby have the power to overcome **any** disease?

But I soon learned that his teachings were quite authentic, because by elevating myself into the illness-curing, subconscious dimension of my mind, I thereby realized that I could completely transcend the physical-level affliction of malaria.

And glory be, by the following morning, although I was still feeling weakly emaciated, I was gratefully able to eat again, and I could even stand up and walk!

Also, to my blissful delight, I felt clear-headed enough to write again, and so I entered the following poem into my bedside journal, a battered little book that I still have today—a collection of sweat and blood-stained memories that contains a verse of mine that says this:

> As I was floating at the entrance of a ((new life's)) gate—
> I realized how to save my body, before it was too late—
> I saw a sparkling ball of light, ((shining)) inside my mind—
> Radiating rays of healing, that became my true ((LIFELINE))—
> And via that (curative) power, I was suddenly revived—
> By ((spirit-linked-energy)), amid which I survived . . .

Alright then, that pretty much describes the [lowest] to the ((highest)) parts of my "out of body," severely tested ordeal in that hospital. All of which was an experience that, quite indelibly, taught me what the eminent Edgar Cayce says in the following truism:

"The spirit is life, and the mind is the builder, and with enough diligent focus on one's spirit-linked abilities, the physical body can be self-cured of any disease that it undergoes."

Thus by realizing the ((ongoing truth)) of that fact, ever since overcoming several near-death encounters in Vietnam, I've been traversing a worldwide search that, piece-by-piece, country-by-country, increases my knowledge about ((self-revival and protection energy)) . . .

As our **New Era, Mind-Over-Body Tour** now moves on to Chapter Three of this book—the section that describes my detailed studies of truly remarkable examples of vibrant longevity, wisdom and amazingly perpetual youth. And after learning about these phenomenal human beings, I believe that you will never forget them.

Therefore, read-on, dear reader, read on, because the best is yet to come . . .

(((CHAPTER THREE)))

LEARNING THE SECRETS OF PLANET EARTH'S MOST AMAZINGLY AGELESS PEOPLE

"What this planet really needs, is more peacemakers,
healers and restorers."
—Dalai Lama

"Once you replace negative thoughts with positive ones,
you will start having positive results."
—Thomas Edison

Yes indeed, after a truly horrendous year in combat-torn Vietnam, upon returning to Pennsylvania, I was feeling especially positive, mostly because I was still alive. But despite the blissful sensation of being a "lucky-survivor," every time that I looked in a mirror, I was faced with the saddening fact that somehow, a year of (life-verses-death, struggling to survive in a war zone) had aged my body fifteen years in one.

Thus due to that depressing realization, yet another crucial challenge began, one that steadily focused me on finding working ways to (((reverse the results of the severe trauma that, in only twelve months, had turned my 23 year-"old" face into looking more like I was pushing 40.

But in the long run, the body-damaging effects of my Vietnam ordeal became a blessing in disguise, because it initiated what gradually evolved into the regeneration-stimulating, self-curing and (protection energy) methods revealed in this unique book.

However, when I first began my quest to uncover the root-causes of physical deterioration, I would soon discover that there was an unfortunate lack of truly helpful information on that subject. As back then, and even more so now, almost all of the "anti-aging" research is done by pharmaceutical laboratories, whereby huge profits are made by selling so-called "skin-saving moisturizers." All of which are creams and lotions that, as I've previously explained, are heavier than water, and thereby cannot be absorbed by skin, a fact that, despite what the ads say, makes buying these products just a waste of money.

Therefore, instead of falling for Big Pharma's "skin-renewal in a jar" scam, to help me discover the actual (mental-plus-physical) **causes** of physical decay, I spent four years in a Philadelphia college, where I took psychology, biology and anatomy courses.

Then, following those years of intensely studying, with financial help from my malaria disability pension, the next step of my studies was to launch myself onto a three-month, fact-finding mission in north Africa—a journey inspired by a magazine article titled:

A Visit to "The Isle of the Ageless"

According to that article, the island of Djerba (pronounced Jerba), a place very near the coast of Tunisia, is home to a rather unparalleled culture that, over time, has enabled thousands of its residents to live an average lifespan that is **two decades longer** than than anywhere else on Earth.

And with the help of my photographic memory, let me tell you about this truly extraordinary, one-of-a-kind island, a place with a lifestyle that is so beneficial to physical longevity, it can an invaluably precious lesson to humanity.

As our **New Era, Mind-Over-Body Tour** now takes us to the turquoise blue, southern Mediterranean, where the ferryboat I was on took me from the Tunisian city of Gabes to Houm Souk, the largest town on Djerba Island. And while I was on that boat, the captain of it, a very friendly, English speaking Tunisian (called Abdul), said to me:

"Well, there she is, beautiful Djerba, the place where I was born, yep, we should be docking there in just a few minutes. And ya know, you're a bit of a rarity, because we don't get many visitors from the United States here, especially all by themselves like you. But I'm glad that you want to write about the very special elders who live on this island, several of whom are well over 115 years old . . . Here, take one of these little booklets, it has some interesting facts about the health and longevity of the people here. Maybe you can use some of this information in your writings."

"And who is this very kindly looking, smiling old man on its cover?" I asked Abdul.

"That is a very recent picture of Yusef Oman, my grandfather. He is the original Zion Temple priest here, the truly honorable, spiritual leader of this island. And believe it or not, just like it says on the first page of that newly updated booklet, he is 121 years old."

"Wow, he is really **that** old?" I said, rather stunned. "He looks amazingly fit and strong for his age . . . So . . . at 121, is he the oldest man on this Island?"

"Oh no, there are three people here older than that, and they are the Burgu brothers, who are age 123, 125 and 128, and all three of them are mentioned inside that little book. And as a matter of fact, according to several longevity researchers, many of whom came here to do studies about Djerba islanders, Yusef, along with the Burgu brothers, are the four oldest people on Earth. And that is the thoroughly verified truth, because the age of Yusef, and also the ages of the Burgu brothers, have been repeatedly validated by hospital birth certificates, along with various other, thoroughly authenticated documents.

"Wow, the four oldest human beings alive, that's truly amazing. I would love to meet Yusef, and those Burgu brothers too. That would be fantastic."

"No problem, my friend, but first I'll introduce you to Yusef, after we dock," Abdul said, while slowly edging that boat into its mooring. "And by the way, Yusef speaks excellent English, and believe me, you can trust whatever he says, because every day, at 7 A.M., he, along with his massive congregation, take a daily vow to devote their lives to honesty and kindness, a vow that is daily recited by the attendees of every Zion Temple on this island. And let me tell you, my friend, by living a life fostered by those basic principles, you are traversing the pathway to a long and healthy, blissful life."

"And that's exactly what I'm here to learn about."

"Well then, you've come to the right place," he said, widely grinning. "And when it comes to seeing an aura-protected, ageless saint, I think that no one here tops grandfather Yusef, mainly because he **really likes** to help people, especially visitors to this island. And if you're looking for a place to stay, I'm sure that he can accommodate you nicely, and probably rent free."

"Alright, that could be just what I need, because I'm currently living on a very small budget," I said, feeling quite uplifted by what he just told me, as I eagerly entered notes about of our conversation into my ever-present, (steadily in my back pocket), notebook/journal.

"Okay, we're securely docked now, so let's go talk to Yusef. He's probably here on the pier, because nearly every day he comes around at docking time, to welcome incoming visitors, shaking their hands and giving them his smile-filled blessings," Abdul said, while turning off the motor of his boat. "**Look**, over **there**, that's **him,** greeting that group of tourists."

As we walked toward the (dressed in white shirt and pants), gray-bearded, Yusef Oman, I immediately thought of the Buddhist priest who I met in Vietnam, as that was the first time I saw someone with the clearly visible, ((radiant aura)) that Yusef so brightly emanated.

And then Abdul introduced me to him, saying: "Grandfather, I want you to meet Jesse, he's a writer, and he came all the way here from the United States, just to do some research about the special culture of this island."

"Oh how nice, that's a long trip," Yusef nodded, cupping his hands together as if in prayer. "I'm very glad to meet you, and I'm especially glad that you want to teach the world about this truly unique, very holy place."

"Yes, dear sir, my purpose on Earth is to learn all that I can, with my classroom being everywhere I am on this planet," I said, while pressing my hands together and nodding, in the same prayer-like way that he greeted me.

"And that is also **my** purpose here," Yusef said, while gently patting me on the back. "So, my young pilgrim friend, if you need a place to stay while you're here, I can help you with that . . . You see," he turned to point his finger at a very large, multi-domed building, sitting atop a hill near the pier. "I am the priest who presides over that temple there. That is my house. And behind that, there are several clean and comfortable, two-room cottages that I reserve for traveling pilgrims, especially those who come from very far away. And at this time, my son, there is an empty one available. So if you're interested in a nice place to stay, free of charge, come with me."

"Okay sure, I'd love to see what you have there," I said, feeling greatly uplifted by the presence of this man who, quite clearly, emanated a sincerely trustworthy energy.

Then, moments later, standing in front of his enormous temple, I was awed by the massive size of its front entrance, a dome-shaped opening that is at least a dozen feet wide, surrounded by a colorful array of inlaid tiles.

And above that towering doorway, there is an inscription that I asked Yusef to kindly translate.

"Yes, that is Berber Arabic," he said, squinting at the sun-reflected mosaic above us. "In English that translates as . . .

You are entering the temple of holy Zion, come and pray amid its genuine peacefulness."

"Oh yes, genuine peacefulness, that's surely what a truly beneficial, non-violent religion is all about," I said, while jotting down his translation of those Arabic words in my notebook. "And I also admire the perpetually open, welcoming entranceway to your temple, one that has no door to close it off from the public."

"Well, the open-door policy is a main part of the Zion Temple philosophy, a sincerely welcoming way of life that is taught at all twelve of our temples on Djerba Island, where we now, all in all, gather more than 22,000 members," Yusef said, smiling while fingering his long gray beard. "And it's mainly due to our island-wide culture of trust in each other, that Zion Temple members have, quite faithfully, adopted the practice of leaving our house doors open, day and night, as a show of faith in the honesty of our holy island family."

And then he told me something quite astounding:

"According to news reports here, due to Djerba's very kind and trustful way of living, for the past nine years, there has been no incidents of thievery or violence here . . . Yes, believe it or not, that's true. And it's mainly because our openly sharing, friendly lifestyle has greatly quelled the desire to steal from anyone, or harm them. Therefore, policemen here usually just hang out in cafes, drinking green tea with friends, while blissfully chatting."

Then, after proudly telling me that, Yusef invited me to walk through the central aisle of his massive temple, where at least fifty rows of cushioned seats are surrounded by intricately beautiful, stained-glass windows that fill the walls.

And then, to the left of its (mother-of-pearl) inlaid podium, (where Yusef delivered his daily sermons), we walked through an archway that led into a huge garden—a lush oasis filled with various kinds of fruit trees and vegetable plants, all of which were vibrantly growing.

"This is the temple's food garden," he said, while waving his hand as if blessing it. "This is where we cultivate just about every kind of fruit or vegetable that we like to eat. And whenever you get the urge, feel free to eat **any** of this food, keeping in mind that it is fresh and safe, because we use no toxic sprays or chemical fertilizers here, only the good black, Creator-made dirt that comes from a nearby riverside . . . But come, let me show you a nice place where you can stay. And later, I will bring you a very healthy dinner."

Then, behind the garden, he showed me a nicely furnished, one bedroom house, with a spotlessly clean kitchen and a tiled bathroom, plus a beautifully hand-carved, wooden table (where I would put my typewriter). And above that splendid table was a large, oval-shaped window, revealing a spectacular view of the Mediterranean Sea. And all of it rent-free, simply because Yusef saw me as what he calls "a truth-seeking, traveling pilgrim."

And just as he said he would, Yusef insisted on bringing me, totally gratis, plates of wholesome food, three times a day, an amazingly gracious service that he continued doing **for the entire three months that I was there**!

Now **that's** what I call **good hospitality**!

Also, due his generous supply of free meals, I discovered the nutritious effects of a semolina type of wheat-grain called "cous-cous"—a rice-like food that is the central source of protein for Djerban people. And along with the wholesome benefits of cous-cous and fresh vegetables, they usually drank healthy beverages such as coconut water or freshly-squeezed fruit juices, plus lots of green tea sweetened with honey. Then, for desert, their favorite treat was a hardy bowl of fresh dates.

And speaking of dates, next to where I was staying, there was a tall date-palm tree that eventually sparked an unforgettable occurrence there, one that began with Yusef saying to me:

"Greetings and good morning, my young pilgrim, book-writing friend, I have a special surprise for you today. As you requested, I will now introduce you to the man who, at 128, is now officially regarded as the oldest person on planet

Earth. And he is also a friend who I've known since I was a child, Mr. Moses Burgu . . . And here he comes now, with several of his relatives, all of whom will verify his age. So, if you want to interview Moses, or anybody in his family, they have no problem with that, because most of them speak English as good as I do . . . Hey brother **Moses**!" Yusef shouted to him. "Don't be shy, come over and sit here at this big table, we have enough chairs here for you and all of your charming family members. Yes, mighty Moses, just have a seat here next to my American writer-friend, Jesse."

Feeling a bit awestruck when shaking the hand of the eminently ancient, Moses Burgu, I was amazed by how spry and healthy he looked, all while being stunned by his radiant aura, a sparkling, golden glow much like what Yusef emanated.

"Pleased to meet you young man," he said, widely smiling while he nodded, revealing a full head of thickly growing, white hair.

And then Moses introduced me to his 109 year-old wife, a very dark-skinned, serene looking centenarian called Sarah. And after jotting her name and age into my notebook (as I did with all of the Burgu family members there), Moses turned to me and said:

"Sarah is my second wife. My first wife, Sabrina, passed away 4 years ago, when she was 116. But let me introduce you to the beautiful daughter of Sabrina and me, her name is Raza, and she is sitting in that chair to the left of you. Daughter Raza recently turned 98, but she still looks mighty good for her age. Raza meet Jesse."

"Well now, it's very rare that I get to meet an American, and such a handsome one at that," Raza said, lifting her hand from the table and softly shaking mine.

"Well thanks for the compliment," I said to her, probably blushing. "And as for you, dear Raza, I can hardly believe that you are 98, because your face is so smoothly unwrinkled. So . . . can you tell me, how **do** you keep your skin so youthful looking?"

"Oh yeah, well, I **do** have **one** wrinkle, and I'm **sitting** in it," she said, and then suddenly laughed. "But seriously now, to answer your question, I've found that it greatly helps to deeply massage my face with the very clean well water here, and so I do that several times a day. And also, I've found that skin is helpfully renewed by drinking lots of coconut juice and green tea. But probably the most beneficial thing I do is, try to learn all that I can about healing knowledge, most of which I get from the teachings of that very special man sitting across the table from you, the truly honorable . . . savior of souls and bodies, Yusef Oman," she said, while respectfully bowing her head to him.

"Well, thank you for that sweet acknowledgement, dear Raza," Yusef said, while beaming his usual grin. "And you really **are** looking stunningly gorgeous these days. So how was your trip to England?"

"Oh very nice, very nice. And as you know, I have a son there who is a famous architect."

And then Raza introduced me to her daughter, slim and sweetly serene Saritah, 64 years old, but still very attractive—a woman who I recently saw singing a solo at one of Yusef's Zion Temple services.

"Saritah is an excellent singer," Moses said. "And so is her very pregnant daughter, Sheba, sitting there across from you, a lovely young woman who represents the fourth, and soon to be fifth, generation of my family tree."

And last but not least, Moses introduced me to his two ancient brothers, Joctor, age 123, and Jacob, age 125—both of whom, along with Moses and Yusef, I read about in the booklet I got from the ferryboat captain.

And then Jacob stood up and inspired what turned out to be the highlight of the day, an unforgettable event initiated by him saying this:

"Well, let me tell ya something, Jesse, even though Joctor, Moses and me are almost as strong as Yusef, none of us would even **try** to do what that amazing man can do. So come on,"

Jacob said, turning to Yusef. "Show Jesse how you can still climb a tall palm tree, and then bring back down a sack of fresh dates. That will **surely** be something he can tell his friends about, when he gets back home. So come on, mighty master of mind and body, how about trying out that extra tall date palm, over there by Jesse's cottage."

And lo and behold, the numerically ancient (but still quite visibly muscular) Yusef Oman shinnied up that tree like it was a casual stroll, and with the same dazzling agility, climbed back down with a knapsack filled with dates—all while the entire Burgu family clapped and cheered.

And then, a bit winded, with his bearded face glowing a bright red, Yusef filled a paper bag with dates, and then handed it to me saying:

"Here, eat these whenever you get the urge for a snack, because there is **nothing** more healthy for your body."

"Okay dear sir, I will surely do that," I said, a bit dizzily stunned by what I just saw him do. "Man oh man, here I am at 27, 94 years your junior, and you can do what I'm too weak and scared to do."

And in response to that statement, Yusef explained to me that agelessness and vitality, more than anything else, comes from "spiritual willpower," a "universe-connected" way of life that was steadily taught throughout Djerba Island.

"Yes, despite the lack of mind-over-body, spirit-linked healthcare that, quite unfortunately, gets pushed aside throughout this planet, we Zion Temple people realize the true importance of progressing ourselves in **evolutionary** ways," he said, while calmly sitting back down at the table. And then he looked intensely into my eyes and said:

"Therefore we don't '**have**' a soul, we **are** a soul, and by truly **living** that perception, we get steadily renewed and protected by developing our spiritual world consciousness. And as to clearly visible examples of our persistent faith in that level of protection, just take a walk through some towns on this island, and you will see that I spoke the truth when, weeks ago, I told you that nearly every front door here is left wide open, day and night. And that is mainly because we **believe** in holy spirits who are **truly** there, keeping us alive and safely guarded, all while they watch over us **continuously**. And by deeply realizing that, belief in spiritual beings becomes far more than a fictitious, ghost story kind of fantasy, but a perpetually helpful reality."

And sure enough, Yusef wasn't exaggerating about Djerba's undying trust in spiritual-level protection, and the following day I saw living proof of it, simply by taking a long hike though several towns there. And never once did I see a front door not left open, even well into the night. Also, several times, when people saw me walking by, although I was a total stranger to them, they warmly invited me into their houses, asking me if I would like a cup of tea, or maybe a piece of delicious (usually date-filled) pastry.

Now **that** is what I call a remarkably ((open-minded)) and trusting way of life. Yes, surely I could go on and on about the truly virtuous culture of that island, a place that inspired me to write a song about it, a little piece that, while being accompanied by bongo drums and guitar, I sang for Yusef and his massive congregation—a heartfelt composition that I call:

Thank You Djerba

Thank you so much for your **ongoing salvation**—
that guides us with **truly spiritual education**—
teaching people about **humane** ways of **sharing**—
teaching us a culture that is based on **caring**—
teaching us how to **truly** live in **peace**—
so that horrible race wars can **finally cease**—
teaching us ways of **joyful longevity**—
ways that are based on **intelligent serenity**—
ways that teach us how to **overcome** greed—
A **peacefulness of mind** that we **REALLY need** . . . .

And yet despite the tranquil bliss that Djerba had developed in me, unfortunately, there was still something sorely missing from my life—a woman who I could be with and cherish. But as for that, my mind remained in love with a women called Julia—a 26 year-old, brilliant beauty who I met in Philadelphia, a woman who shared my fervent desire to be a mind-over-body researching, globe-trotting book-writer. But after a year of steadily seeing each other, our love affair sadly broke up, mainly because neither one of us was ready to commit to a very serious relationship.

And after writing Julia a letter from Djerba, during my third month there, I got a rather stunning reply from her that said this:

"Dear Jesse, I really miss you badly, and I hope you will soon come back to Philadelphia. By the way, after you left here and went to Djerba, you motivated me to do some traveling. And so I recently spent two weeks in South America, and while in Ecuador, I met a very famous, 118 year-old, Incan healer who, quite amazingly looks HALF that age. And he can also do some real and TRUE spiritual magic, and surely he would make a fascinating addition to your work-in-progress book. And if you want to interview the truly phenomenal Pablo Yupaqui, just come back here, and I will buy us two round-trip tickets from here to Quito, Ecuador, so we can visit him. Okay?"

And indeed, that was an offer I could not refuse, especially since seeking out amazingly ageless people was then, and continues to be, a major theme of my writings. Therefore, a few days after getting that deeply motivating letter, I decided to say fare-thee-well to magical Djerba Island, and I was soon on a ferryboat back to mainland Tunisia, where I would catch a jet to Italy—followed by a long flight back to the Philadelphia airport.

And glory be, Julia was there waiting for me, and quickly gave me a big hug, followed by her bubbling excitement about the month-long, research trip that we would soon take—a journey that would intensely enlighten our lives.

As we now move our **New Era, Mind-Over-Body Tour** again westward—to where the snowcapped Andes Mountains tower over lushly green, equatorial jungles—to the gorgeous country of Ecuador, the place where Julia and I learned about:

Tapping Into the Incan "Secrets of the Ancients"

What intrigues me the most about the Ecuadorian, Incan culture are two things: its widely unknown (but truly powerful) methods of plant-based healing, and the fact that archeological studies reveal it to be one of the original civilizations on planet Earth, one that is over 10,000 years old.

And after taking three planes to get from Philadelphia to Quito, Ecuador, Julia and I then took a long and winding road, four-hour bus ride that took us to the mountainside town of Macas, where Pablo Yupaqui often gave healing ceremonies.

Called in guidebooks "The Emerald of the East" (due to its location on the eastern slopes of the central Andes), Macas is a lush, extremely green jewel of panoramic views like I've never seen anywhere. And being that it was almost sundown when we arrived there, quite exhausted from our long trip, Julia and I immediately checked into a small hotel, and quickly collapsed into sleep—figuring that we would look for Pablo in the morning.

And just as if it was meant to be, early the next day, outside our hotel window, in the park across the street, a small gathering of people were standing by its fountain. And sure enough, Julia quickly recognized Pablo Yupaqui as being in the center of that group.

"That's **him**!" she shouted. "Come on, let's get dressed and go talk to that truly fantastic man. And trust me, Jesse, you will **soon** realize that it's well worth coming all this way to meet and be with him."

Then, after excitedly bounding down the stairs, we walked to the center of that park, very anxious to talk to Pablo. And immediately I was stunned to see how young he looked, this beardless man with shoulder length, black and white streaked hair, a kindly faced, intelligent looking fellow who looked like he was no more than 60.

"Buenas dias, it's so good to **see** you again!" Pablo shouted, while walking toward Julia. And after giving her a warm embrace, he turned to me saying: "And who is this handsome young fellow with you, a traveling researcher-writer like yourself?"

"Yes he is, and his name is Jesse . . . And I'm sure that he will . . . eventually be a very famous author," she said, while softly holding my hand. "And he came with me all the way from Philadelphia, just to meet and interview you."

"Fantastico," Pablo said, while beaming a wide smile. And then he turned to Julia, saying: "Well, now, it seems you can't resist returning to this truly beautiful place. And as to what you said in that letter you sent me, apparently you and your companion would like to experience one of my . . . Vision Quests."

"Yes, we have a plan to do that," she said, nodding to Pablo. "And if it's okay with you, Jesse wants to write about that . . . ritual in a book he's putting together, a book about the mind-over-body powers of spiritual energy."

"Okay sure, no problema, I'm here to help anyone on the path of vital knowledge," Pablo said, while touching the necklace of small orange flowers that encircled his neck. "And even though you are half Peruvian, and know the Spanish language very well, to help Jesse write about my teachings, I will keep our conversations in English. Okay then . . . if you people are ready for it, we can do a Vision Quest tomorrow morning. But as I told you before, this experience involves a two-hour hike into those mountains . . . to the west, to a very special, spirit-linked power-place called Mayta. So, my children, be sure to wear some comfortable shoes for the long trail to get there, Okay? Just meet me here in the plaza at 8 a.m., and we will do that . . . soul-reviving trip. And please, in the morning, before we go, don't eat any breakfast, because when we get to

Mayta, if it's okay with you and Jesse, all three of us will be drinking a mixture of some very therapeutic herbs, an ancient, spirit-connecting medicine that we Incans priests call . . . ayahuasca."

The whole time that Pablo was talking to us, one question kept entering my mind: even though Julia showed me newspaper and magazine articles about him (one of which was titled: "The 118 year-old, National Treasure of Ecuador"), could he **really** be **that** old and yet, in some mysterious way, maintain the looks of a very fit 55 or 60?

Anyway, fervently trying to keep up with Julia's steady flow of positive energy, I heartily agreed with her plan to do what Pablo called a "Vision Quest."

"So, I will see you two amigos tomorrow. Just be here at the plaza at 8 a.m., and although I don't wear a watch, I'm rarely ever late for an appointment," he said, smiling while holding up his deeply veined, bare wrist. "And so I **will** be here at 8 o'clock, Sky Spirits willing. Hasta manana . . . and do try to get a good night's sleep, to build up your energy for that . . . rugged hike."

And with that said, he walked back to the group of people waiting to speak with him, as they patiently stood there by the fountain.

Then, after returning to our hotel room, while Julia and I ate some breakfast, I spoke to her about Pablo's plan for us to take the powerful potion called ayahuasca (pronounced "i-a-waska"), voicing my concerns about what I heard is a very potent drug.

"Well, according to Pablo, it's an ancient medicine that people have been taking for centuries," Julia said. "And although I've never taken it, I believe that it's safe enough for us to . . . give it a try. And also, it could be an interesting experience to put in your book, because, for one thing, I've been told that ayahuasca can be very rejuvenating, as it strongly connects one's mind and body to what Incans call . . . 'The Energy Field of the Ancients.' So I suppose it could be . . . beneficially life changing. However, I've also heard that ayahuasca sessions are safer, and much more therapeutic when it's guided by an Incan spirit-connector, and Pablo Yupaqui is very famous for being that."

"Okay then, maybe we **should** try it, at least **once**," I said, "Especially if it can do all that you just said."

"Yes, **maybe** it can do all that . . . and I'm very glad that you'll be with me when we take it. Anyway, it could be a fascinating memory that we can share," Julia nodded, while puckering her lips and giving me a soft kiss.

Then, later on, while she was soundly sleeping next to me, before I dozed off into dreamland, I did some mind-energizing, Inner Directions that would help to sharpen up my photographic memory, preparing it for what I expected to be a very memorable day, and indeed it was surely that.

And the next thing I knew our alarm clock went off at 7 am, followed by us quickly getting ready for our trek into the mountains with Pablo.

"Remember hon," Julia said while getting dressed. "We're not supposed to eat any breakfast this morning, so our stomachs are fairly empty before taking the ayahausca, because sometimes it makes people nauseous."

"Yeah, but I've read that the nausea quickly goes away, and then the blissful part of it kicks in," I said. "Anyway, surely we will need something to quench our thirst along the way, and so I'm bringing three pints of purified water in my backpack . . . Okay then, with our water needs taken care of, if you're ready to go, my precious love, let's do one of . . . Phenomenal Pablo's Vision Quests."

And sure enough, true to his word, when we entered the park at 8 o'clock, he was already there waiting for us. But before we launched into our journey to his "power-place" in the mountains, Pablo turned to us and said:

"Do you see that very old, white painted adobe building by the edge of the plaza there, the one with a sign on the front that says Macas Hospital de Vuestra Merced? That is the first hospital built in this town, and it's also where I was born, way back in 1854. And in case you people have any doubts about how old I am, you can check with the hospital records there, if you feel the need to verify my 118 years of living in Ecuador."

"Ah come on Pablo," Julia said, "Every where I've been in this country, people know about you, whether it be from your TV interviews, or the articles about you, or your nationwide healing tours. So of course, Jesse and I didn't come all this way just to be with someone who's not the genuine, real thing."

"Well now, I'm very glad that you folks comprehend that, because the truth is, I-man Pablo Yupaqui am a living and breathing, Earth-walking miracle. And it's mainly because of what I have right here," he said, tapping his forehead with his fingers. "Yes, my children, the essence of my perpetual youth is mainly the outcome of what I call . . . Mystical Psychology. And today, my young and comely compadres, you may learn some truly helpful pointers about the body-re-creating energy that's **in** and **all around you** . . . Alright then, if you people are ready, let's move forward into this . . . adventure. Did you bring some jackets for the cold air up there?"

"Yep, we've got jackets, and I've got three bottles of clean water, right here in my backpack," I said. "Two for Julia and me, and one for you, if you need it. And I've also brought us some apples."

"Well, that's nice, but I've got food and a water jug, here in my shoulder bag. And also, to perk us up, I've brought my bamboo flute," he said, while flashing that wizardly gleam in his eye, much like what Yusef Oman emanated, but for some yet to be known reason, Pablo looked at least two decades younger than him.

"Alright then, let's get trekking," he said. "And try your best to keep up with me, because I'm a long-time, professional walker, and I walk **very fast.**"

As we then proceeded to follow him through the cobble-stoned streets of Macas—all while dozens of people looked out from doors and windows, waving at him and shouting "**Viva Pablo!**"—as he waved and hollered back.

And then, not far from the edge of town, suddenly there was nothing but a wilderness of trees, divided by a narrow, rocky path that led up into much steeper mountains. And it was on that upward climb that Pablo, quite skillfully, played his bamboo flute while walking, resonating his soothingly, high-pitched melodies, tunes that were sublimely suited for that altitude, where glistening, snow-capped peaks towered high above us.

Then, after about an hour of hiking through that dreamlike scenario, we took a break, during which Julia and I sat down on some boulders, sipping water and catching our breath. All while Pablo remained standing, intently eying a huge eagle that soared directly over our heads.

"How magnifico," Pablo said, widely smiling while he looked into the sky. "That's an Ecuadorian, Holy Alapo eagle. Yes, see how easily it soars on the Spirit Wind. He can hover like that for hours and not get tired. And having long-studied the energy of eagles, I have found that by . . . imagining that I'm soaring like one, I can walk for hours without getting tired, especially when I'm up here on this trail. And to help you folks deal with the stamina it takes to hike in this high altitude, both of you should try doing that. Yes, just picture yourself flying like an eagle while you walk, and that will make this trek a **lot** easier." And then he gleefully mimicked the giant bird above us, waving his arms up and down like wings, and then he shouted "Oooweeeee!"—a sound that was amazingly ((echoed back)) by the eagle that soared overhead.

"Hey! Did you **hear** that Alapo screech like that?" he shouted. "He's telling us that if you imagine that you're soaring like **he** is, you can use the **wind** as a motor that keeps you gliding!"

"Oh yes, I can see that you a tirelessly soaring, magical eagle for sure, especially with that beak-like nose of yours, almost as big as mine," I said, feeling increasingly giddy from the thinness of the air. And then I reached into my pack to offer him an apple.

"No thanks amigo, I don't want to eat any fruit now. But I do want to have a taste of those apu-apu flowers over there, just like the ones around my neck, but up here they grow much bigger, and they are quite delicious."

And then he walked over to a small tree covered with orange, rose-like blossoms, saying: "Now **that's** my favorite snack," as he stuffed his mouth with several of them, chewing their petals while shouting "**delicioso!**"

"These are very special Ecuadorian apu-apu, and I just picked enough to sweeten the taste of my ayahuasca recipe," he said, after sitting next to me. "These precious flowers will help its flavor and aroma. But the most important part of the mixture is the ca'api vine, what we Incan healers call the Spirit Vine, some of which is growing up ahead . . . over there by those small, vine-covered punga trees. So that's our next stop, where I can collect some leaves of that . . . very powerful plant."

Then, after he put a few handfuls of "Spirit Vine" into a woven bag, after we steadily hiked for another half-hour or so, Pablo turned to us and said:

"On the other side on that at hill, up ahead to the left of us, is the little town of Tranquilo, a favorite place of mine. But I haven't been there for awhile, because I just spent two weeks in Macas doing healings. And right about now, I'd like to pick up some groceries at the outdoor market there . . . And then, a few miles past Tranquilo, is our destination, the holy village of Mayta. I have a house there, where I live with my wife, except for when I'm out on the road, doing healings. And after we get to Mayta, I will cook us up some ayahuasca. Then, after we each drink a cup of it, the three of us will combine our minds and spirits, and that enlightening process will culminate the mission of this . . . Vision Quest. So, in case you people are wondering about our schedule, the pretty much it, Okay?"

"Whatever you say, my friend. You are the boss of this trip, so just take the lead and we will follow, no problema," I said. "And ya know what, for the past half-hour or so, I've been imagining that I'm a soaring eagle while I walk, and it really

works! I'm feeling much stronger now, and the altitude up here is no longer tiring me out. And what a good feeling that is, a whole new boost of energy!"

"And the eagle-soaring thing is working for **me too**!" Julia said, while taking off her straw hat, and shaking loose her long black hair. "I'm feeling much less dizzy now, and less short of breath."

Then, on his tirelessly gliding wings, Pablo guided us into the Tranquilo marketplace, where several people rushed up to him, shaking his hand, and giving him warm hugs.

And after Pablo bought some herbs and vegetables there, we said our "hasta luegos" to that friendly little town, followed by winging our way up the rocky trail to Mayta.

"Ah yes, there she is, at the top of that big hill to our right, my holy power place, magnifico Mayta," Pablo said, eying that tiny village with a smile. "So you two keep your eagle wings a-flapping, because the trail that gets us up there is pretty steep."

And very soon both the altitude and the view took my breath away, when we came upon a truly splendid sight: a group of small waterfalls that cascaded at least hundred yards straight down, pouring its dozens of streams into a pool of crystal clear water.

"This gorgeous, stream-filled gorge is made by melted snow from the top of Mount Capac, that brightly sparking peak looming there, high above us." Then, after telling us that, while holding his hands together as if he was praying, Pablo bowed to that amazingly glowing mountain. "Yes indeed, it's mighty Mount Capac that supplies my house with what we drink and bathe in, because a stream of this very pure water is piped into an elevated tank in my backyard, flowing from there into our indoor faucets. And so I call this group of waterfalls, El Regalo de Los Dios, which translates as Great Gift from the Gods. But if you want this precious liquid straight from its source, just fill up your canteens with it, because there's nothing better for renewing your health and stamina than purely clean, fresh from a mountaintop water."

Then, following that delightful stop at Pablo's "Great Gift from the Gods," water supply, we hiked up the path that soon brought us to his house. And after passing by the fruit trees and vegetable gardens that surrounded it, when his adobe-walled dwelling came into view, Pablo stood in front of it, saying:

"Yep, that's my very old but still sturdy, home-sweet home. And those Incan designs that I painted on it, they help to energize the food that we grow here, while they also protect my wife and I from harm. Alright, there she is now, at the front door, my sweetly beautiful wife, Ma-on. **Ma-on, estoy aqui!**" he shouted, followed by him walking up to her, where they warmly embraced on their doorstep.

"Ma-on, meet Julia and Jesse," he said, turning to us. "They came here all the way from the east coast of North America, just to do a Vision Quest with me."

"Oh how nice, that's very a long trip," she said, beaming a smile while shaking our hands.

And then Pablo briefly conversed with Ma-on in Quechua (the ancient dialect of the Incans, a language that, according to archeologists, is the oldest vernacular on Earth). And following that, he faced us and said:

"I was just telling Ma-on that both of you are very good, open-minded people. And to increase your faith in what we Incan healers can do, I will now tell you a few things about this amazingly lovely, 88 year-old wife of mine . . . Okay, first of all, her long black hair has never been dyed, because she steadily energizes its inborn color. And as to the youthfulness of her face, you can be sure that it's not a result of surgery or injections, but it's the genuine outcome of the metaphysical and herbal methods that she and I, over the years, have developed. And as you can clearly see, Ma-on looks at least three or four decades younger than her numerical age."

"Yes, dear people, my husband only speaks the truth, even though I sometimes get a little embarrassed when he brags about me," Ma-on said, slightly blushing. "But surely no one knows this amazing man better than me, having been married to him for over fifty years now. Yes, a half-century that, again and again, has proven that Pablo is an authentic, true-to-life healer, a man who can **really** change your life for the better."

"Well thank you for the compliment, my love," Pablo said, while putting his arm around the stunningly youthful Ma-on. "But right now, I'm sure that Julia and Jesse must be tired from that rugged hike. So come on inside you two, and rest your feet, while I get busy cooking up some sacred brew."

As we soon discovered that the inside of that house was just as unique as its colorfully painted outside, because quite unlike the stiffly square angles of wood-based framing, the adobe-formed entrances to its bedrooms were oval shaped, with curtains instead of doors. Also, its living room walls had painted renditions of trees and flowers that Pablo, quite skillfully, had created—all of which gave that place a rather cozy, organic-style feel to it.

"Yes, there's nothing like the perpetual emanation of art, especially when it reflects what the Creator of Nature blesses us with. And by what you've done with your walls here, I see that you truly realize that," I told Pablo.

"Yes, part of my passion to decorate this place, comes from realizing that an adobe house lasts much longer than a wooden one, and it doesn't require killing trees to build it," Pablo said. "In fact, even this cushioned chair that I'm sitting on, as you can see, is made of adobe and not wood . . . Yes, we Incans deeply respect trees, because they contain the oldest spirits on Earth, many of which keep growing for **thousands** of years, a duration that makes even my age seem very brief. In fact, one of the ingredients of my ayahuasca, holy tea recipe comes from the bark of the giant lopuna tree, a phenomenal being so ancient that, some of them have been around since the days when Moses walked the Earth."

And then he told us that the best time to drink the "holy tea" was after sunset, because it often makes one's vision very sensitive to light.

"So until gets dark outside, why don't you two just take a nap in that bedroom there, the one on the right, next to ours.

And then, in the early part of the evening, we will begin the Vision Quest ceremony."

"Whatever you say Pablo, your wish is our command," I said, while again jotting down notes about his proclamations in my journal.

"And by the way," Ma-on said. "While you two lovebirds are resting, by deeply inhaling some breaths of the pristine breeze that comes through that bedroom window, that helps to clear your minds for the healing effects of Pablo's . . . very special brew."

Thus taking her advice, we laid down and did some deep breathing of the cool breeze there, all while being awed by the luminescent, sun-reflected view of snowcapped Mount Capac.

Then, after resting for a few hours, feeling delightfully revitalized by breathing in the purity of that mountain air, Pablo stood at the bedroom door and said:

"Okay you two, it's now time to expand your self-healing powers, because my spirit-connecting, ayahausca tea is ready to drink. So, please come into the dining room, where the three of us can sit at one table."

And then, after putting on a ceremonial hat that had red, green and yellow patterns sewn into it, Pablo put three ceramic cups on the table in front of us, and then filled them with a reddish-brown liquid, poured from a teapot that was decorated with Incan symbols. All while Ma-on sat on their living room couch, intensely watching us.

"Amid the spiritual glow of the twilight, and the holy, inborn powers within us, we will now partake in this ancient healing ceremony, a ritual that begins with this chanted prayer, one that I will now recite in the sacred language of Quechua," Pablo said. And after a few minutes of singing that enchanting invocation, he again sat at the table, and then quickly drank his cup of ayahuasca. "Okay, now the two of your drink yours, drink all of it." And so we did, somewhat nervously swallowing what, to me, tasted like very strong, unsweetened chocolate.

Then, amid the candlelight that softly illuminated the room, Pablo played his flute for a while, until he leaned back in his chair and said:

"In a few minutes, when the spirit of the holy tea starts to come on strong, I will describe to you the deeply healing purpose of this potion," he said, followed by him continuing to play his bamboo flute.

And after several minutes of listening to his soothing melodies, I began to feel the effects of what we drank.

At first it felt like a tickling flutter of energy, starting in my stomach and running up into my head, a sensation that compelled me to close my eyes.

"Julia," I called to her. "Please tell me if you see the glowing ball of light that I'm now seeing inside me, it looks like a radiating spiral that is . . . somehow filling my body with a tingling sensation."

"Okay sure," she said, "I'll take a peek inside and see what's up." And after several seconds of watching her in silent, eyes-closed meditation, she smiled and told me this: "Yes, I do see a spinning vortex of light in there, and it gives me a nice feeling, like my body is totally . . . glowing inside."

"That radiating light is what we Incan healers call your Internal Sun, it comes from the very center of your mind, and it is your central source of self-regenerating energy," Pablo said, while leaning back in his chair. "Yes, one of the wonderful things about ayahuasca, is its power to tap-into a clearly inward look at your spiritual Body of Light, the visual essence of what steadily re-creates every molecule of your flesh and bones. And in a little while, I will show you what that very powerful emanation can do, an amazing ability that, hopefully, you will never forget."

"Wow," Julia said. "When I focus on that ball of sparkling light within me, I can feel my heart throbbing, like it's . . . somehow **dancing** in my chest."

"Oh yes, I know that corazon bailando feeling well. It's a natural effect of ayahuasca awakening your body," Pablo said, while again flashing his radiant grin.

"Okay then, that explains it," she said. "Instead of a dancing heart, I'm feeling what Spanish words call . . . corazon bailando . . . As again I realize how Latino phrasing can make even . . . scary sensations sound so gently pretty."

"That's because Spanish is the language of love, a dialect that mixes well with Quechua, especially when the poetry of Latino phrases merges with the spiritual potency of Incan culture. Yes, and speaking of the power of Incan culture, now that the ayahuasca has helped you merge with central-brain, healing energy, it's a good time to test your powers of self-renewal," Pablo said, leaning forward while placing his dark, vein-covered hands on the table. "Okay . . . right now I want each of you to tell me something that may require a minute or two of contemplation. I want you to tell me if there is . . . anything about your body that you want healed or changed. Maybe it's a lingering physical injury that is painful, or maybe you have some unwanted wrinkles on your face, or a scar that you wish could be erased . . . How about you Julia, is there anything about your body that you would like to be able to heal or change?"

"Well Pablo, now that you've brought it to my attention . . . a little over a year ago, in Philadelphia, I got hit by a car that cracked a bone in my right arm," Julia said, pausing while she rubbed her elbow. "And it's been hurting ever since, giving me pain every time I move it."

"Okay, in a minute or two, I'm going to help you fix that," Pablo said. "And how about you, Jesse, is there a bothersome ailment that you would like to heal? If so, tell me about it."

And after thinking a little while about his request, I said:

"Well, although I'm only 28, there are deep wrinkles on my face that make me look much older, most of which is trauma-caused, facial damage that I got from being drafted into a war in Vietnam. And even though it's been over five years since I went through that long and terrifying dilemma, I still get angry about what that nightmarish year did to my face, along with the . . . brain jangling flashbacks I get, every time I think about what happened there. Anyway, maybe you can . . . somehow heal up some of the mental and physical wounds triggered by being in that . . . miserable conflict."

"Oh no, I can't heal you, that's **not** what I do, because my central aim is to teach people to steadily heal **themselves.** Yes, my friend, that's the way **real** self-renewal works, mainly by tapping into your Internal Sun, metaphysical powers. And that is the main reason for taking ayahuasca, because it greatly helps people merge with the potently healing abilities of their subconscious mind . . . But let me explain the basics of how this medicine works . . . First of all, it helps to realize that, largely because of the stress-loads and traumas of life, your regeneration powers tend to weaken, whereby they gradually lose the central-brain, healing-connection that subdues physical and mental decay. However, after administering ayahuasca to **hundreds** of people, I have found that, only **one dose** of it, **if** effectively guided, can perpetuate a stimulation of the brain's regenerating powers that, for many of my Vision Quest patrons, has lasted for decades. But the ongoing effects of the holy tea mainly depends on one very important process, and that is how firmly you **believe** in your self-healing abilities. But unfortunately, most of that belief gets suppressed by the profit-based, medical industry, mainly because mentally powered self-curing is a major threat to the outrageously high prices charged for so-called . . . healthcare. And yet amid the Incan ways of healing knowledge, by being open-minded enough to try it, people **can** achieve new levels of self-repairing abilities, and thereby greatly expand the durability of their brain and body."

Then, after hearing what Pablo said about the long lasting, mind-over-body benefits of ayahuasca, I felt duly compelled to ask him this:

"But if this . . . holy tea, knowledge-expanding medicine is as perpetually healing as you say it is, why isn't it more widely used, because outside of Ecuador and Peru, not many people seem to know about it?"

"Well, my friend, that's largely due to the long established, Incan tradition of keeping ayahuasca as a **truly sacred** part of a religious ceremony, and to sell it would be something like a Catholic priest selling cups of wine at a church held, communion service. And so we Incan ministers try to keep this . . . potion from becoming a profit-based, problematic thing. Therefore, as far as I know, ayahuasca has **never** caused a fatality. And that is probably because it's not a synthetic chemical, but instead it's a healthily organic drink, a beverage made mainly from two Nature-based ingredients: the juice that comes from the leaves of the ca-api vine, along with boiled pieces of bark from an ancient Iopuna tree. And so it's strongly linked with the perpetual energy of natural re-creation. And of course, your body is also perpetuated by natural re-creation, steadily renewing itself for as long as your regeneration system keeps working. And quite thankfully, Ma-on and I are truly blessed, ongoing examples of a perpetually regenerating way of life . . . Alright then . . . now that you realize the body-renewing, profit-free nature of what I do and represent, we will now move on to the next step of the Vision Quest process. And to initiate that level of consciousness, I want the three of us to form a healing-energy-link, doing that by joining our hands together, so that we surround this table with our connected emanations."

Then, after we initiated what Pablo called "The Hand-Holding Circle of Life," he leaned forward and said:

"Okay, now that healing energy from our fingers is flowing through the three of us, let us bow our heads while I recite this brief, but vitally crucial, Vision Quest prayer, an invocation of thankfulness that, when translated into English, goes something like this:

"Dear Creator of Life on Earth, thank you for the inborn, regenerating energy that enables me to overcome all forms of disease and decay of my precious body . . . as I again recite a very grateful prayer for the blessing of perpetual health and life."

And after several seconds of silence, Pablo said: "Okay then, now that I've shared my nightly prayer with you, let us now move on to the next step of the Vision Quest process . . . as we will now direct our attention to the three-pronged candle-holder at the center of this table, because it's here for a couple of reasons. First of all, its trio of flames symbolize the three of us as a singular unit of healing energy . . . And along with that, those candles are here to provide enough light for **you**, dear Jesse, to clearly see your face in that mirror, there on the wall behind you. So go ahead and stand up, and then carefully look at your reflection. And then tell me if you can see any evidence of the facial crevices that you wanted removed, because just as I expected, the holy tea has sparked your ability to continually heal trauma-caused, mental and physical effects."

And sure enough, after closely examining my candlelit face, I could clearly see that, to my shocked surprise, it re-energized the youthful, wrinkle-free look that, before my year in Vietnam, I felt lucky to have.

"Good god, Pablo. How **did** you change my face like that?" I said, truly astounded.

"I **didn't** change it, and neither did the ayahuasca, **you** are the one who sparked the healing emanations from your mind, truly potent energies now **developing** within you. Yes, it' all part of what I call . . . The Universal Reality."

And as for Julia's damaged arm, that too was amazingly healed during our dream-like (but true-to-life) session with phenomenal Pablo Yupaqui, whereby the lingering pain in her arm was ((permanently)) cured.

But along with penetrating his famously effective methods into our brains and bodies, the morning after his Vision Quest ritual, Pablo taught us some truly vital knowledge that (with the help of my journal and photographic memory), I will now describe.

It was a day that began with us having breakfast with Ma-on and Pablo, sitting on their backyard patio, surrounded by a sun-reflected, golden crown of snowcapped peaks.

"Yes indeed, I never get tired of seeing the emerging dawn rise up over these mountains," Pablo said, while he contentedly leaned back into his colorfully painted, adobe-formed chair. "And with enough Internal Sun energy flowing through us, I'm steadily grateful that, every morning, we wake up inside a newly regenerated body, just as sure as sunlight makes a new day rise again."

"Well, thanks to you Pablo, it's **surely** a new day for me, now that the . . . lingering ache in my arm is totally gone," Julia said, looking more ((pain-free)) happy than ever. "Yep, it's as good as new now . . . And by the way, how about Jesse's new face. Wow, he looks ten years younger than he did yesterday. And much more relaxed."

"Yes, dear amigo, thank you **so much** for what you've done for us. You are **the real thing** for sure," I told him, and truly meant it.

"Nah, it's not about me being real, it's about the reality that you people are now **able** to create. And then, if you get the urge, both of you . . . obviously bright people will **teach** what you have learned . . . But as for now, go ahead and enjoy the nice breakfast that marvelous Ma-on has prepared for us."

As we then eagerly filled our empty stomachs with sliced mangos, papayas and apples, along with large portions of freshly baked cornbread.

"And also, try some of these vitamin-packed nuts that come from the sacha inchi plant," Pablo said, while pointing to a bowl of them. "They are seeds as big as peanuts, but they are far more nutritious. Yes, sacha inchi seeds are a gift from the Ecuadorian jungle, a truly beneficial super-food."

(Note: The many healthy effects of sacha inchi seeds are listed at the Wikipedia.org website).

Then, after we ate and conversed for a while, I took some pictures of the exquisite view from their patio.

"Yes sir, I've been a lot of places, but here in your backyard, you have the most magnificent scenery that I've ever seen," I said, while eying the mountain-rimmed, lushly green valley, shimmering there, over 10,000 feet below us. "And with these photos that I just took of this superb piece of paradise, later, when we go back to the States, I'll pick the best one to make a nice painting of it."

"Oh really, you're a landscape painter?" Pablo asked.

"He's a **brilliant** landscape painter, Pablo, he does gorgeous murals that are very realistic, but he also adds his own spirit-linked style to them, making them unique," Julia said, followed by me saying:

"Yeah . . . I've been painting my version of nature scenes ever since I was a small child, and I even won a few art contests, back when I was only eleven or twelve years old. And ever since then, I think that I first learned to paint during a . . . previous incarnation."

"Nice . . . Hey, maybe I can help you with that," Pablo said, again beaming me in with his intensely penetrating eyes. "Last week, when I was in Macas, I was visited by a good friend of mine, an expatriated Englishman who lives in Quito. His name is Charley, and he owns a very nice, famous restaurant just outside of that city—a place that he named Peace on Earth. And about a week ago, I brought Charley here, and he said that my backyard view is so fabulous, that he wishes he could have a nicely painted, mural of it, one that would spread across the front of his restaurant. And then he asked me if I know a talented landscape painter who could do that job. And so I told him that I'd send him a good artist to do that. Anyway, because you people plan to head back to Macas today, and then back to Quito on a bus, when you get to Quito, you could take the photos of this view to Charley's Peace on Earth place, and tell him Pablo Yupaqui sent you to do the mural that he wants."

And then he wrote a note for me to give to Charley—Pablo's personal recommendation for me to be the one to do that painting.

"And along with that, while you're creating that piece of work, you and Julia could probably stay in one of Charley's motel rooms there, free of charge," Ma-on said. "Yes, he is a **very** generous guy, and will probably pay you well for that mural. And also, I'm sure he will gladly feed you people some good food."

"Alright, that sounds great to me," I said, "And if Charley wants me to do that painting, I will surely try my best to do a skillful work of art. Thanks for telling me about that, brother Pablo."

"You're quite welcome, I'm glad I can be helpful to you people. And by the way, I will accompany you two on your hike back to Macas, because this afternoon, I'm scheduled to do a healing ceremony, in the plaza there, where we met."

"Okay **great**, we can again spread our eagle wings and **soar** back to Macas **together**," I said, feeling very relieved that he would be with us on that rugged hike, because I never met anyone who can arouse people's energy like he can. "But Pablo, there's something that I've want to ask you about these . . . Vision Quest sessions. Do you always do them for free, no pay at all?"

"Well, as I mentioned earlier, we Incan priests believe that we carry forward the original civilization on Earth, and as examples of the healing powers of our culture, Vision Quests are not done for money, but for the precious gift of being blessed by holy spirits," he said, while giving me a soft pat on my back. "And as you can see by looking around here . . . we grow **lots** of food, and so quite fortunately, we are self-sufficient. And sometimes, to help us out with a little cash, Ma-on sells some of our fruits and vegetables, just down the road, at the Mayta outdoor market."

And then, after a brief period of silence, with a serious look on his face, he said:

"Julia and Jesse, now that you've got me thinking about it, let me give you people some good advice about Quito . . . Okay . . . when you go back there, be very careful not to do too much riding around in taxicabs, because in that crazily, rapid-paced city, the cab drivers race around like speed demons, and are famous for getting into accidents."

And then he told us about the time when, while he was riding in a taxi in downtown Quito, he got into a very serious smash-up.

"Oh yeah, that was one of the most traumatic ordeals of my life. As there I was, up front with the driver, when suddenly that car was moving **so fast,** he lost control of it, and then he crashed it into a big truck, one that was parked on the side of the road, hitting it **so hard,** its tail-gate broke loose and **smashed** through our windshield! But fortunately, neither one of us was hurt, mainly because I had the wherewithal to **see** that accident coming . . . Yes, I had just enough time to evoke my spirit-linked, energy barrier, a transformation powerful enough to launch that driver and me into the metaphysical dimension. Oh yes, it's true, by merging with the aura of your Internal Sun, when necessary, you can strongly shield yourself, and other people too, by expanding what we Incan healers call Rayku-Pura, the emanation that radiates from what we call The Spiritual Body of Light."

And then, while standing up and stretching his muscular arms out to his side, he went on to say: "Believe me, when I tell you about the vast abilities of expanding the Internal Sun's Rayku-pura, I'm telling you the **truth.** But of course, I realize that this kind of . . . metaphysical power seems somewhat unbelievable, especially now, when knowledge about truly human abilities is being pushed by aside by pharmaceuticals and such, causing us to lose touch with our most vitally protective skills. But the way I see it, the best thing that can happen to humanity is, quite diligently learning about the fourth dimension of the human mind, whereby people can finally advance onto a truly progressive, spirit-linked level of self-curing and physical protection."

"Yes Pablo, I totally believe that myself, especially after experiencing what happened to me when I was drafted into the Vietnam War. Because after spending a year in that bloody nightmare, I got so feverishly stricken with malaria that, while laying in a hospital bed, I saw myself as a . . . departing spirit, hovering over what seemed to be my . . . lifeless corpse, somehow transcending it. And it was then that I realized that there is not only one but **two** of me, my physical self, and also my soul-level, spiritual dimension. And then, by **reconnecting** my metaphysical body with my physical body, I was able me to overcome a very deadly strain of malaria."

"But Jesse," Pablo said, while gently putting his hand on my shoulder. "I hope you realize that these frightening, death-defying tests happen for a **crucial** reason. Because probably the most effective way for people to believe in spiritual-level transformations is by first **experiencing** them, and then, urged by that momentous discovery, seeking out ways to learn about how that . . . higher dimension shift is evoked. But unfortunately, **truly** genuine teachers of the metaphysical realm are few and far between."

"Yes, that's so true. And that is why we came all this way to learn from **you**, dear sir. And I'm very grateful for the experience of being able to write about what you have taught us."

"Yes, you a truly wise and noble spirit," Julia said, while giving Pablo a warm hug. "And your spiritual wisdom will be forever planted in my memory."

"Well, it's been my sincere pleasure to have you people as my guests, and I deeply respect the open-mindedness of both of you," he said, while standing up and stretching. "But if you two want to catch the twelve o'clock bus to Quito, we should pack up and get hiking back to Macas. And then, up north, when you get to Charley's restaurant, just give him that note I gave you, and show him the pictures you took of my view here. And I'm sure he will take my advice, and pay you to do that mural, one that I'm sure will greatly brighten up that area."

And then, just as I expected, Pablo made the long hike back to Macas memorably uplifting, especially while his flute playing kept us ((soaring)) above the rocky ruggedness of that trail.

Following that, after two days in Quito, Charley's restaurant mural project was delightfully begun, whereby I spent a week depicting Pablo's Mayta view, blissfully spreading it across the front of that very large building.

And then came the finishing touch: the restaurant's "Peace on Earth" title at the top of the mural, a name that I encircled with brown, yellow, red and pink hands—((racially-united)) hands that spread across the top of that (hopefully) peace-and-Nature-promoting piece of work.

Thus thanks to Pablo, I created my largest and most widely viewed painting, and surely the nicest. And it was also nice that Charley paid me a thousand U.S. bucks for a project that I would have done for free, because I find it both physically and mentally therapeutic to paint ((heartfelt)) depictions of natural beauty.

As I will now wrap up this ((permanently painted in my memory)), Ecuador adventure with Pablo's farewell message to Julia and me:

"Adios amigos, vaya con Dios, and be sure to follow the path of the truly spirit-connected, deeply conscious mind and body . . ."

And duly following his advice, from there onward I would try to stay steadily aware of what he called "Expanding Aura, Internal Sun Powers," increasingly believing in (and thereby developing) the potentials of that vastly significant dimension.

As we now shift our **New Era, Spiritualized Mind-Over-Body Tour** to eastern Arizona, where, a few years after leaving Ecuador, I learned some vital facts about the Native American, Apache version of ((protection-energy-forces))—a phenomenon that they call:

"The Body-God's Shielding Spirit"

During the winter of 1976, I drove from Santa Cruz, California to the mountainside town of Eden, Arizona, inspired to go there after reading a very interesting article about the 77 year-old Zi-yay, daughter of the legendary Apache Chief and medicine man—Geronimo.

That National Geographic magazine article was titled **"Geronimo's Daughter, Zi-yay: The Amazingly Ageless**

Goddess of the Southwest." And after reading about Zi-yay's captivating philosophy, along with seeing her photograph, I was convinced that she was someone truly worth interviewing—a woman who was not only overflowing with wisdom, but also, despite her age, she was amazingly beautiful.

And after setting up a question-and-answer session with Zi-yay, although it took two days to drive to her house, it was truly worth it, especially after she helped me defend myself from what, quite shockingly, could have been a crippling gunshot wound.

But before I share with you the Zi-yay interview that eventually led up to that ((bullet-shielding)) test, l will transcribe some of the amazing history of her Apache tribe—along with uncovering some extraordinary facts her very unique father.

First of all, I should emphasize that, according to archeological research, before their 400 miles-wide domain was conquered by the U.S. Cavalry, the Apaches ruled over it for nearly two thousand years, a duration that makes them the original inhabitants of the area now called Arizona.

But as is evident throughout history, indigenous people are "traditionally" overrun by foreign armies, a situation that, quite unfortunately, keeps their [strictly material world] invaders ignoring the oftentimes, beneficially ((Creator-linked)) knowledge of highly spiritual people.

And surely it was fourth-dimensional, spirit-world connections that enabled the Apaches to withstand one of the bloodiest conflicts in worldwide history—the U.S. Cavalry versus The Apache Nation War, a continuous battle that lasted four decades, roughly from 1856 to 1896. All of which was a ((spirit-power-versus-firepower]] war that waged the massively equipped U.S. army against so-called "unruly savages" who, by living in open-air villages, could easily be wiped-out by guns and exploding cannonballs.

But mainly due to chief Geronimo's guidance, to avoid being easily trapped and slaughtered by rifles and artillery, the Apaches shifted their lowland villages to the forests of very high mountains, a tactic that greatly increased their chances of survival.

And yet despite their uncanny ability to withstand decade after decade of full-scale war against them, in typically "enemy"-demonizing style, newspapers kept calling for increased military actions against Geronimo's so-called "vicious barbarians."

But if the truth be told, before being forced to defend themselves against a myriad of genocidal-aimed attacks, the Apache culture was traditionally nonviolent, so much so, that before killing even a rabbit for food, they would ask their "High-God Usen" for forgiveness.

However, to keep his tribe from being totally eliminated, books about Geronimo steadily point out that, when it comes to overcoming the forces of superior weaponry, no one was more cleverly tactical than he, "The Chief of Chiefs." But of course, from a U.S. military point of view, instead of seeing Geronimo as a heroic figure, he became widely publicized as "Public Enemy Number One"—a designation that, in the long run, caused him to receive bullet scars on nearly every part of his body. And yet according to reports about him, Geronimo healed himself "unbelievably fast"—a so-called "supernatural" capability that, quite amazingly, enabled him to live 79 years.

But let me share with you a newspaper account of Geronimo's history-making invincibility, a March of 1878 article in what was then called The Arizona Times. And according to that front-page report, a U.S. Cavalry captain was quoted as saying this about the "The Undefeatable Chief."

"The 45 caliber bullet that I saw hit Geronimo, hit him directly in the center of his chest, the same place where his famous "Apache Shielding Symbol" was painted on his skin. But to my shocked surprise, that powerful bullet just bounced off him, and only made a tiny scratch!"

Further yet, history books say that along with his renowned ability to withstand gunshots, no prisoner-of-war cell could hold Geronimo, as he continually escaped to his "sacred hideouts"—many of which were atop Arizona's (10,700 foot high) Mount Graham. And it was amid that mountain's massive forests where Geronimo initiated what he called "Closing the Door," a tactic that had tribal members camped in hidden lookouts, amid which they could see for miles, whereby no army could do surprise attacks against them.

Thus "Geronimo's Last Stand" went on and on like that for decades, a mode of survival that many Native American tribes came to regard as a piece of "heroic history." And upon discovering a book that contained some Apache songs about their most famous leader, I found this especially potent line that, when translated into English, says this:

"Oh greatly mystical Geronimo, hold up the dawn, and we will sing to it!"

But despite his world-famous, unyielding tenacity, four decades of anti-tyranny, nonstop rebellion eventually took its toll on Geronimo's body. And after making his ninth escape from a prisoner-of-war cell, while spending the especially cold winter (of 1909) atop snowcapped Mount Graham, he was deeply afflicted with a severe case of pneumonia. Then, after a long battle against that disease, while he (and two dozen of his still surviving tribe) were being attacked by the U.S. Cavalry, a soldier found Geronimo's fever-stricken, severely weakened body laying in a tent-covered bed, whereby he was easily captured. And then two soldiers tied him up, and after carrying him down that mountain, they put him into the back of a wagon, followed by Geronimo being taken on a very long, winter-rainstorm drenching trip that eventually brought him to a jail cell at Fort Sill, Oklahoma.

And it was there [after two days of again being locked up], on the 17th day of February, 1909, the incomparable Chief finally surrendered his war-torn body—launching himself forward onto the (English word version) of what Apaches call "The Energy-God Promised Land."

And to duly honor the most legendary man in the history of North America, I will hereby contribute to the list of songs about him, doing so by sharing this one that I wrote about him, a verse of which goes like this—

> If I ever get to The Promised Land—
> I will gladly shake Geronimo's hand—
> Hoping that he's happy at his new destination—
> Where he's finally free from oppressive invasion—
> Where wars about race will never take place—
> Where he will never again face that disgrace—
> Where his Powerful Spirit roams free from fears—
> Reuniting with friends, and welcomed with cheers . . .

And with that said, I will now commence with the taped interview that I did with Zi-Yay—the amazingly wise and ageless, 77 year-old, Apache tribe survivor who, at that time, lived in a house on the slopes of her father's favorite hideout, where she greeted me by saying this:

"Well hello there, you're here . . . So . . . you must be Jesse, the healing-energy exploring writer. Yes, it's nice to meet you," she said, while warmly shaking my hand. "And by the way, I'm very impressed by the sample pages that you sent me of your . . . work-in-progress book. So . . . come on inside, and let's get this . . . little interview powwow started."

And then she hummed a tune while we walked into her adobe-walled house, a place with a tall, curvilinear ceiling, and thickly textured walls—all of which were beautifully decorated with her paintings.

"Wow, ever since I saw that article with photos of your artwork, I've been anxious to see them up close, yes, they are truly unique," I said, feeling immediately mesmerized by her colorful renderings—a myriad of dreamlike landscapes filled with eagles, owls and butterflies, while hovering above them were ((radiantly glowing)) people with wings on their shoulders. "Yes, I really like the way that you interact human beings with creatures of the sky, brilliantly depicting the coexistence of people with the spirits of Nature."

"Well, I'm glad to hear you're an art lover like myself. But come and have a seat in the kitchen, and have a glass of iced tea, surely you must be thirsty after driving through the desert," she said, while pushing back her long, jet-black hair from her face, silky tresses that went all the way to her waist.

Then, while sitting there, sipping her sweetly, honey-flavored brew, I placed a battery-operated tape-recorder on the table between us, figuring that for this interview, I wouldn't just take notes, and fill in the details later. And after asking her if it was okay to record our conversation, she said:

"No problem, go ahead and get that thing taping, so we can help to enhance your . . . obviously well intentioned book."

"Alright then, well . . . not surprisingly, the first thing that comes to mind about you is . . . how amazingly youthful you look for your age. Because according to National Geographic magazine, you are 77, and that's a publication well known for being factual. And also, your 1899 date of birth is mentioned in articles about your father's life. But for goodness sakes, somehow you've managed to sustain the appearance of a very lovely . . . 30 or 35. So . . . to satisfy my curiosity, am I being too forward by asking you **how** you've managed to become a famous icon of ageless beauty?"

"Okay . . . first of all, let me begin by emphasizing the fact that I've **never** been operated on by a surgeon's scalpel, nor have I received any injections, or any other gimmicks used by the . . . so-called 'mainstream' medical industry. But instead, I use self-induced, spiritual, mental, physical and dietary ways that **really** subdue the aging process. And by steadily focusing on truly genuine ways of self-renewal, I've come to realize that, more than anything else, humanity needs to put **much** less emphasis on fantasy and trivia, and far more focus on what **really** matters to our personal well being. And by practicing a continually learning, effectively self-curing way of life, the process of minimizing the mental and physical challenges of . . . growing older becomes, quite essentially, our **number one** priority."

And then, after pausing to poor me another glass of her deliciously strong, green tea, she said.

"But of course, needless to say, diet and daily exercise deeply effects what we've come to call . . . ongoing rejuvenation. Although most importantly, from my standpoint, I steadily align myself with the perceptions summed up by a favorite prayer of mind, one that, long ago, my father taught to me. And it says basically this . . . As I look back toward my past, I am filled with gratitude that I am still alive. And as I look toward the sky, I am filled with the magnitude of spiritual power. And as I look toward the forest and wildlife, I merge with the energy of endless creativity. And as I look toward my future, I deeply envision an ever-renewed, ever-stronger me."

"And what a truly memorable prayer that is," I said. "Yes, and as to the part about creativity, surely your painting skills are deeply involved with that. So . . . being a longtime artist myself, can you share with me any clues about how . . . creative energy effects the mind and body?"

"Wow . . . that's a very complicated question to answer, Jesse, because the art-making process has a countless number of dimensions to it, so many facets that, good heavens, whole books could be written about the effects of creativity on our mental health. But as to one of the therapeutic results of painting pictures, I have found that it greatly helps people maintain what I call . . . a sense of placement. And as most, so-called 'elderly' people eventually realize, our sense of placement tends to wither with age, and that's why, as we get older, we often forget where we put things, even if it was only a few minutes ago. But thankfully, ever since I took up painting, my placement-sensing, memory banks have gotten much stronger . . . But anyway, far beyond re-energizing our short-term memory, by activating the creative reservoir within us, we can learn to utilize body-protecting abilities that, if focused on, can take us to new levels of self-empowerment. For example . . . back when I was a child, I clearly remember my father teaching me to paint what he called the Apache

Shielding Symbol, a colorful design that was put on the forehead and upper chests of the twenty-four tribal members who, at that time, lived in our mountaintop village. And as a regular ceremony, every morning, the two dozen of us would gather into a circle, and while holding hands, we would chant a song aimed at arousing the spirit-linked, protective effects of the injury-shield symbols painted on us. And then, after a few minutes of that chanting ritual, we would reverently bow our heads, while father Geronimo recited a prayer of heartfelt thanks to the mighty Sky Spirits, the eminent beings who, again and again, enabled us to survive."

"Zi-Yay, please, let me tell you what I'm feeling right now," I said, deeply entranced by what she just told me. "When you described that scene of your tribal members holding hands while your father bowed his head in prayer, I could **clearly** see him doing that, almost as if his spirit is right **here** in this room, watching us."

"Yes . . . every day I can feel the power of his thought-waves. And right now, I can feel him sending you a welcoming message, mainly because your seem to be a **true** believer in his . . . sacred abilities. And due to your strong urge to spread knowledge about the spirit-linked realms of healing and protection, by connecting with me, his cherished daughter, his powerful energy will probably protect you as well."

"Oh yes, I'm a true believer in Geronimo's metaphysical powers, especially after reading two books about his life. And both of them kept emphasizing the monumental fact that, for several decades, it was **his** leadership that kept your tribe from being totally wiped out."

"And I'm sure he appreciates the fact that you realize that . . . And by the way, as to my father's Apache Shielding Symbol," she said, standing up and pointing to one of her largest paintings. "It's featured there, radiating in the center of that . . . angel-filled sky . . . But let me explain the various parts of the Geronimo designed, sacred shielding symbol. First of all, the green circle represents the eternal powers of Nature, and the purple X in the middle of it, expresses our passion to spiritually protect ourselves. And the red dot in the middle of the X symbolizes the innocent blood that will spill, **if** we let a bullet, or anything life-threatening, pierce our precious bodies . . . Thus much like what the shielding power of the cross represents to Christians, I remember my father saying that all protective symbols come from what he called . . . The Center of a Soulful Life. But unfortunately, when it comes to what emanates from the center of one's being, most of humanity has been turned away from tapping into it, mainly because of the notion that people should not be too . . . so-called 'self-centered.' But the way I see it, if you're not '**self**-centered,' then where **is** your center? Inside a rifle bullet? Or a television set? Or a cannonball fired in the heat of battle? . . . And yet by keeping my spiritual wisdom centralized within me, I've become much more guided by what makes me mentally and physically stronger."

"Yes, there's no doubt about it, dear Zi-yay, you've lived a uniquely tested and very creative life, and you are **truly** blessed with beauty-preserving energy, inside and out, an emanating glow that gives you the most . . . brightly shining aura that I've ever seen."

"Well, thank you for that nice complement. And speaking of life-preserving energy, take a look out that window, there behind you, where my yellow van is parked," she said, while standing up. "Do you see that slightly dented, Shielding Symbol that I painted on the driver's side door?"

"Sure, I can see it, and although it's been a little bit scratched-up, it's still a nicely rendered version of that design."

"Well, believe it or not, just a few months ago, while I was driving that van through downtown Safford, a guy in a pick-up truck, doing at least at least 50 miles-per-hour, came roaring through a red-light, and just plowed right into the door that symbol is on."

"Wow . . . And that little dent is all that happened, after being slammed into by a truck?"

"Yep . . . pretty amazing huh. And neither me nor that guy who hit me was injured. And that's yet another result that I figure was . . . mainly energized by my father's ever-protecting spirit."

"And not only that, but I'm sure his life-saving emanations have also helped shield you from the effects of so-called . . . time."

"Well, young man, I'm very glad that you can understand what I'm all about, a realm of knowledge that they don't teach in college. Yes, and I often wonder **where** are the so-called 'universities' that educate teach people about the spiritual **universe within** and **all around us**? Okay sure, conventional college courses can help people communicate with each other, or solve various mathematical or biological problems, and maybe even enable them to get a job. But **where** are the schools with teachers who are **genuinely** effective metaphysicians, schools that educate people about truly significant, life-saving levels of consciousness? Where are **those** schools, Jesse? . . . But anyway," she said, while lightly putting her hand on mine. "I'm glad that there are people like you around, someone who, even at the tenderly young age of 32, already has a decade of metaphysical studies in his brain. And let me tell you, the main reason why I invited you here, was because I was very captivated by those pages you sent me, giving me a potent sample of what . . . truly open-minded human beings are capable of learning. And after reading about those amazingly ageless Tunisians, and then, good heavens, the part about that miraculous human being, Pablo . . . wow, it's easy to see that you have a very bright future ahead of you, a powerful destiny as a truly revealing author."

"Well . . . coming from a person who has a wall filled with highly conscious books, your belief in my literary potential means a lot to me," I said, somewhat blushing from her deeply memorable feelings about my work.

"And after we finish this interview, which of course, I hope your readers will find educational, I think you should write a piece about another truly spirit-linked, Native American, the one who is called Rolling Thunder, a man who many say has supernatural abilities that are truly astounding," she said. "And according to what I read about him, he got the name of Rolling Thunder after, in front of many witnesses, he channeled-in a spirit-evoked tornado, a phenomenal feat that he conjured-up in the middle of the Nevada desert, at a place where it wouldn't damage any people or structures. But what that amazing tunnel-of-wind **did** do, was give a huge crowd a momentous view of what a Native American chief can do, both as a way of demanding respect, and also a reminder of the . . . far too long overlooked connection between the spiritual world and Nature. All of which is a force that can either massively create or destroy, depending on how well its treated . . . And now, duly so, the mighty Rolling Thunder is the new leader of the Shoshoni tribe."

"Oh yeah, that amazing man is known worldwide, and I recently read a book about him. And I'm fairly certain that he is a person who, much like your father, is someone strongly linked to what Apache and Shoshoni culture calls . . . The Sky Spirit Energy Gods. Also, according to an article I read, Rolling Thunder's glowing aura is so visible that, a group of Buddhist monks came all the way from Tibet, just to witness his luminescence."

"Yes, I also heard about that," Zi-yay said. "And surely he's another one who deserves a part in your writings. And he can be easily located, because he usually stays at his house in Carlin, Nevada, unless he's traveling around, doing public appearances."

"Okay, maybe after I return to California, I'll take a trip to Nevada to visit him," I said, ever ready to connect with truly spirit-linked, transcendently conscious people.

"Alright then. But if you go to Rolling Thunder's place, make sure it's when he's not on one of his many touring trips. Because right now I hear he's part of a shebang that Bob Dylan calls The Rolling Thunder Revue. Yep. he's getting to be quite the celebrity, that's for sure. And a few months ago he opened up a bunch of shows for the Grateful Dead . . . But anyway Jess," Zi-yay said, quickly standing up. "It's getting late in the day, and I'd like to get to the Safford Market before they close at 7. So . . . I would like to wrap-up this visit by saying that I've really enjoyed your presence here, and I think you are a truly wonderful, wisdom-filled soul. And may good spirits keep guiding you, ever forward on your quest to learn the vital secrets of . . . life versus death. And always remember that **true** love of your body is a river, a clear-flowing river hat runs long and deep, steadily connected to its healing energy."

And with her invaluable truisms permanently imprinted in my mind, I gave Zi-yay a nicely long, good-bye hug, an embrace that briefly culminated my feeling that she is one of the most gifted, creatively spiritual people on planet Earth.

And then, freshly revitalized by her glowing aura, I took off in my rattletrap Dodge van, bouncing back down that mountain road and on into the sunset-lit desert—motoring back to the motel where, early that morning, I rented a small cabin.

As I will now draw this chapter to a close, to make way for the one that, to a large extent, focuses on the extraordinary results of what I've come to experience as true-to-life, ((Spirit-Linked-Protection-Energy)).

Thus the next section of this book begins by transcribing what happened the same evening that I left Zi-yay's place—an unforgettable gunshot incident that, with the help of (metaphysical powered shielding), I was able to minimize the effects of a 45 caliber bullet wound.

Yes indeed, there's no doubt about it, amid this steadily discovering, spiritually tested, mind-over-body journey of mine, it seems that I'm inevitably destined to encounter, clarify and teach a multitude of ways to overcome injury, disease and decay. And so again I say, read on, dear reader, read on, and ((hopefully)) realize that, quite honestly and authentically, my aim is to share **truly** beneficial facts of life . . .

Or as the great, twentieth century artist, Grandma Moses said (at the age of 101):

"Life is like a camera, if you focus on what is truly important, you can capture clear pictures of uplifting factors of consciousness" . . .

(((CHAPTER FOUR)))

TRUE-TO-LIFE ACCOUNTS OF ((SPIRIT-LINKED-PROTECTION-ENERGY)) REVEALED

"Either write something worth reading,
or do something worth writing about."
—Benjamin Franklin

"If you help enough people get what they want out of life,
you can also get what **you** want."
—Nelson Mandela

Upon arriving at the The Healing Waters Motel (a place named after a nearby hot springs), I was greeted by a fellow who rented a cabin next to mine, a man who I had a long chat with that morning—a half-breed Navajo named Clarence Coyote. And after I stepped out of my van, he walked over to me and said: "So . . . how was your visit with who the local newspaper calls . . . The Ageless Miracle?"

"Wow, what an extraordinary woman, she's not only looks amazingly half her age, but she's also brilliant and gorgeous," I said, still buzzing from eying her luminescent beauty.

"Oh yeah, she's something else alright," Clarence said, smiling while he folded his arms. "So anyway, this morning you said that you might want to go with me to Crystal Pond, to check it out. And because this is going to be a full moon night, we can see **lots** of wildlife out there, including owls, hawks, coyotes and jackrabbits. So come on, jump into my Chevy pick-up and let's go. I've got a twelve-pack of beer in there, and a bucket of French fries. And at the pond, we can shoot us a few fat jackrabbits, and then later, my wife will make a delicious bunny-barbecued stew. So maybe you might want to join us for that meal.

"Well, as for shooting rabbits, nah, I'm not into doing that," I said. "I just want to see what kind of . . . wildlife is happening there, because I heard that Crystal Pond is a very special place."

"It **is**!" Clarence shouted. "That area has more wild critters than anywhere else around here. And it's only a quick little, one-hour trip for us to go out there and back."

"Okay then," let's do it," I said, not yet realizing that this "quick little trip" would soon turn into the painfully complicated ordeal that I call:

((Spirit-Linked-Protection-Energy)) Test 1: The Bullet-Shielding Test

By the time we got to Crystal Pond, the moon was full and bright, shining on the water like a beacon. And it was there that Clarence turned his headlights off, and after he shut off his truck, he softly said: "Shhh, keep your voice down now, so we don't scare the animals away."

And sure enough, within a few minutes of being there, a couple of jackrabbits were visible in the moonlight, two of them running from a pair of coyotes when, quite quickly, an owl dove at one of the escaping rabbits, and then flew away with it.

"Wow . . . it **is** like a nature movie out here," I whispered, suddenly feeling excited, because I've always been a wildlife observer to the core.

"Okay now, do you see that big jackrabbit there, just sitting by that cottonwood tree?" Clarence asked me.

"Yeah, sure, I see it, especially since the moon is glowing in his eyes."

"Alright . . . now this is my trusty, silver-plated 45 magnum," he said, grinning while he pulled a shiny pistol from his glove compartment. "And this . . . costly piece of hardware has a very easy to pull, hair trigger, so it don't jump and spoil your accuracy when you shoot it. So . . . you wanna try to plug that big old, juicy-meat rabbit with it, the one just sitting there dazed, like he's waiting for it. Come on, Jess, grab a hold of this pistol and let me see some of that Vietnam vet, warrior-hunter style in you," he said, while trying to hand me that gun. But I quickly pushed it away, figuring that it was time to give Clarence a dose of true-to-life, Vietnam reality. And so I let him know this:

"Hey man, about me and that war, I was no so-called 'hero' over there. In fact, when I was ordered to shoot people, most of whom were just poor farmers trying to survive, instead of doing what the other guys in my platoon did, quickly blasting them, I just shot up into the air. Yeah, because **my** plan was to keep my conscience **clear**, see . . . Okay, sure, I saw a lot of death and dying in that jungle, but I stayed **totally** against that politician-ordered, needless war. So I never shot **anybody,** not there or anywhere else. And that's nothing but the truth. And as to the huge amount of casualties involved with that . . . insanely useless, Vietnam disaster, accurate statistics reveal the fact that, of the more than 50,000 of our soldiers who died there, at least **half** of them were killed by American bombs and artillery. Oh yeah, I saw **way too much** of our own exploding stuff gone-blooey, whereby somehow, it was stupidly dropped on **top** of our own units."

And after telling him basically that, I asked Clarence what I see as a truly significant question about war:

"Anyway, think about this: what with all the self-destructing mistakes going on via our military invasions, who is the **real** enemy, them or us?"

And then I told him that, instead of killing so-called 'gooks' in the Nam, I spent a lot of time trying to **learn** from them, trying to figure out **how** the Vietcong were beating the most well-equipped army on this planet.

"And so . . . ever since then, I won't even touch a gun," I said, quite earnestly. "So don't even ask me to shoot any of these . . . wild rabbits out here, because for one thing, they are the crucial food of owls, hawks and coyotes, and by killing what they eat, we destroy the vital balance of Nature."

"Ah, come on man, you sound like a wimp," Clarence snarled. "Don't ya know, guns are a part of **real life** here in Arizona. And it guns that kept us Navajo's alive, back when soldiers were trying to wipe out my mother's race."

"Okay, I get what you're saying about that. But there was a lot more to Native American survival than weapons. Because just like Zi-Yay said, Apache lives were saved mainly by the energy of . . . spirit and willpower, the kind of potent wisdom that Geronimo taught, and what Zi-yay teaches **now.**"

"Well, as for me, I don't much cotton much to all that wizardly . . . mumbo-jumbo that she believes in. But I'll tell ya what, this here gun is a Smith and Wesson, a finely tuned tool with such an easily pulled trigger that, when I shoot at one of those ol' jacks out there, even at 50 yards away, I can hit it in the head. Yeah man, guns are what feeds us, and keeps us free from thieves," he said, while taking another swig of beer. "So don't be a pussy, and just hold it for a minute, just to feel its mighty firepower."

And although it was totally against my better judgment, I let him hand me that gun, just to show Clarence that I wasn't afraid to hold it. But as soon as I got a grip on that damn thing, barely touching it—**BLAM!**—its hair-trigger **fired**—shooting a bullet that went straight through my left knee—followed by it tearing a hole through the floor of that truck.

"Whoa!—I **told** ya about that gun's sensitive trigger, god-**damn** man," Clarence shouted. "You **shot** yourself and you're bleeding like **crazy!**"

Oh yes, I was bleeding alright, and very scared that I shattered my kneecap. "Listen, this wound hurts like hell, so don't rub it in, okay? Just take me to the nearest hospital, or whatever you have here, in this area."

"All we have is a clinic in Safford," he said. "So I'll just take ya there. But hold on tight now, cause I'm gonna drive **real fast**!"

And he surely did, racing down that bumpy road like a speed-demon, just missing trees and boulders by a few inches. All while I tried to slow down my loss of blood, doing that by keeping a tourniquet-like, pressure-grip on the thigh above my knee, tightly squeezing the arteries there. Also, I tried to stay very **calm**, because I remembered seeing men in Vietnam die from the heart-racing, "shock" effect of a heavily-bleeding wound, even if it only penetrated an arm or leg.

Then, after painfully limping into the Safford Clinic, I was glad to see that there was a nurse on duty—a nice lady who immediately bandaged my knee. But along with that, she said that I should go to the nearest hospital (which was in Tucson, a 90-minute drive).

"Oh yes, you better go there," she told me. "Because the bullet directly entered your kneecap, and probably fractured it. And that could be a injury which could permanently impair your ability to walk."

And so of course, worried about how much damage I had done, perhaps a crippling injury, I agreed to do what she said. But because the clinic's ambulance was being repaired, she asked Clarence if he could drive me to Tucson.

"Sure, no problem, let's **go**!" he shouted. And so we took off in his super-charged truck, racing at a crazy 80 miles-per-hour all the way to the hospital.

But on the way there, to deal with the throbbing ache in my knee, I steadily utilized what I call **Expanded Awareness Pain-Cling Release**—an effective way to help ((mind-powered endorphins)) do their agony-relieving thing. What happens with this method is, I hypnotize myself by ((**deeply** focusing)) on something the Creator of Nature made, such as a tree, or a mountain, or perhaps a big cloud, or a river. Or what was very prominent that night, the brightly shining, full moon.

Then, after about an hour of being mesmerized by the moon's brilliant glow, whereby my tormented knee was mentally overpowered, suddenly my (pain-quelling, self-hypnosis) was interrupted, when Clarence stopped the truck, and said:

"Okay, we're here, right next to the Tucson General Hospital emergency room. So come on, hang on to my shoulder, while I help you walk in there."

Thus with Clarence's help, I limped into that dreary ward, all while whispering prayers to my spirit-linked, body-god, hoping that I was somehow shielded from being crippled by a stupidly, self-inflicted accident that I might long regret.

But lo and behold, soon my fears of crippling myself were joyfully relieved, because the examining doctor there told me the wonderful piece of good news that, according to their X-rays, **no bone damage** was done to my knee.

"And it's hard for me to believe it, because . . . look here," the doctor said, pointing to my bandaged knee. "See the blood spots there on the bandage, they clearly show the bullet directly hit the inner side of your kneecap, and then exited on the other side of it. And so, with a point-blank, 45 caliber gunshot like that, it seems . . . impossible that your knee bone hasn't been shattered to smithereens."

And then he told me that, if my kneecap was shattered, they would have to replace it with a manufactured, plastic one, and that would cause a lot of difficulty with walking.

"But in your case, well, I'll be damned," he said, scratching his head. "**Somehow**, the bullet **bounced-off** your knee, and then went . . . amazingly **around** it, exiting here on the other side—giving you only a superficial wound, a result that is quite . . . unexplainable. Yes sir, you are one **lucky** fella, someone who pulled off just some kind of miracle."

And after putting a fresh bandage in my knee, that doctor (while still shaking his head in disbelief) said:

"Well . . . Mr. Lucky, all you need to do now is, try to stay off that leg for a while, which will help it to heal up. And of course, you need to pay your bill, at the nurse's desk, there across the hall."

Then, after paying for the X-rays and the doctor's fee, I gleefully limped out of that hospital, so glad that I wasn't seriously hurt that I shouted **YIPEE**—hollering my thanks for the "miracle" of ((shielding-energy)).

Yes indeed, and what a tension reliever that was. And as a memorable reminder of the ((protective emanation)) that was somehow potently evoked, the (entry and exit scars) of that bullet will, again and again, continue to verify the supposedly "unexplainable" outcome of that incident.

As I increasingly realize that no matter what it's called, whether it be the forces of the "Body-God's Shielding Spirit," or the (("Internal Sun")) radiations of brainpower, its name is unimportant, because labels are not what makes (protection energy) work. But what **IS** important about this significant level of consciousness, are efforts to spread the truth about its multitude of potentials, whereby they don't get ignored [or covered-up].

Therefore, to help humanity learn about the vastly unexplored realm of ((metaphysical)) transformations, this chapter describes several true-to-life experiences that I call Spiritual Energy Tests—all of which involve truly remarkable incidents of being protected from serious injury.

And as to the healing of that self-inflicted bullet wound, the day after I left that hospital, while laying on a couch at The Healing Waters Motel, trying to stay off my feet before I drove back to California, Zi-yay came by for a visit. And then, while she held her hand a few inches above my wounded knee, humming a tune while she emanated her ((healing energy)), she told me this:

"Being shielded from a gunshot wound, so that it didn't cripple you, well, believe it or not, the fact that shot yourself was no so-called . . . accident. Because more than anything else, it instigated an important message from your body-god, one that will urge you to believe in your spirit-linked powers, especially those involved with injury protection and . . . rapid healing."

And speaking of rapid healing, sure enough, the day after Zi-yay's visit, to my stunned surprise, I was already able to walk without feeling pain. Thus I felt quite ready to get back on the road again, and so off I went, gleefully driving back to my cozy bayside apartment, east of San Francisco.

As our **New Era of Mind-Over-Body Tour** now moves on to California's Santa Cruz Mountains, the place where, in 1979, three years after my trip to eastern Arizona, I would again intensely test my (protection-energy) abilities. But this time I would encounter an incident far more lethally dangerous than a bullet in the knee—an experience that, to this day, remains to be the most truly phenomenal, (injury-transcending) episode that I've ever been through.

And although the following occurrence may seem to be very difficult to believe, this is a **totally factual, completely unexaggerated** account of what happened on that winter's day west of San Jose—this the surely ((life-saving event that I call:

((Spirit-Linked-Protection-Energy)) Test 2: "Miraculously" Unhurt Amid a Car-Demolishing Accident

Mainly because it's one of the most progressively educational cities in North America, in 1979, I decided to rent an apartment in Berkeley, California, where I would live for two years. And during my first month there, I met Tony Mendel, a well known reggae singer who I would soon become friends with, followed by me (occasionally) chanting back-up vocals (while also playing conga drums) in his band.

And then came that Sunday afternoon when Tony and I were terrifyingly tested, a momentous day that began when he asked me to go with him to a very important event—an anti-nuclear-power rally that featured the world renown Bob Marley and the Wailers. But quite unlike the stadium-filling concerts that Marley was known to pull together, this one was held at an open field, high up in the mountains between Santa Cruz and San Jose.

Thus being a devoted admirer of "Natural Mystic" Marley's very conscientious, timeless songs (that I've been listening to ever since 1970), I quickly agreed to go with Tony on what he called "a joyride to reggae heaven."

However, that "heavenly joyride" soon turned into a traumatic journey to hell and back, shifting from pure terror to uplifting ((bliss)). And so let me tell you about the stunningly ((spirit-connected)), twists and turns of that day.

After about a one-hour drive in Tony's (somewhat dilapidated), Pontiac station wagon, while on a mountain road filled with very sharp curves, when a downpour of rain made the road very slippery, I got somewhat nervous about how fast he was driving. And so I asked Tony to **please** slow down.

Who me, drive too fast? I do **everything** fast, it's a habit I got from my father," I remember him saying—a remark that made his (ringed with curly blond hair), somewhat angelic face turn quickly angry, whereby he took on a a very nervous, somewhat nasty look.

And then, when I realized that the 65 miles-per-hour [which he seemed very locked into] was far too fast to handle the oncoming turns, I looked for a seatbelt to put on, only to find that his (very old car) didn't have any. As it became increasingly clear that if Tony didn't ease up on the gas pedal, we would soon slide off that dangerously wet road, but for some (inherited from his father?) reason, he failed to see that.

Therefore, for safety's sake, I figured it was time for me to somehow, at least **try** to evoke the (protection energy) that Pablo and Zi-yay taught me about. And so I did some deep breathing, while (intently focusing) on arousing the ((dimension-shift)) that dematerializes bodies—the injury-shielding process that Vietnamese Buddhists call "The Spirit Wind from Within."

And then, while I was earnestly hoping to evoke some spirit-linked help, we came upon a big, pond-sized puddle in the middle of the road, about six inches of rainwater that caused Tony to step hard on the brake pedal—a maneuver that made his car skid sideways. As suddenly we were gliding off the side of the road, and then rolling over, **upside down off a steep cliff!**

And although what happened next is difficult to believe, it's a clearly seen rerun in my memory banks.

While we tumbled down that very rocky incline, that vehicle's hood got torn off, causing pieces of its motor to smash through the windshield—as fragments of engine parts and glass flew past our faces ((**somehow** missing us))! And then, after several seconds of being barraged by chunks of broken glass and steel, finally that crumpled wreck came to an abrupt stop, sizzling there at the bottom of a gorge.

Then, while laying inside that upside-down station wagon, semi-unconscious, I remember feeling like my time to ((pass-on)) had come, and I was soaring onward into the afterlife—readying myself for a newly reborn incarnation.

But after slowly waking up from the coma that enveloped me, I lifted my hand, and then suddenly realized that my body was **still alive**. And then I saw Tony move his legs, as he slowly uncurled from the bundled-up, fetal position that he was in, while blinking his eyes.

And then, after both of us gradually awakened from that brain and body-shocking ordeal, we then checked ourselves for injuries. But to our stunned amazement, neither one of us was seriously hurt, and between the two of us, all that we got was a few minor scratches, one on Tony's right hand, and two small cuts on my right wrist—an outcome that was truly unbelievable.

However, after smelling the gasoline that was leaking from the busted-up, petrol tank (directly above us), we knew it was time to quickly exit that vehicle. And so we crawled through the [[completely demolished]] windshield, followed by us nervously backing away from that pulverized Pontiac, totally astonished to see how destroyed it was.

"Nah, this **can't** be possible," I remember Tony saying. "Are you **kidding** me? We just went through all that, and the only injuries we got was a few small scratches?"

Then, after saying that, Tony started shivering (inducing what often happens to someone in a state of shock). And to calm his nerves, I told him to sit down on the large boulder that was next to us, and then take some deep breaths, which he did. All while I kept thinking about how blessed we were by life-saving, protection energy.

And then, to expand his comprehension of what we just experienced, I reminded Tony about the book I was writing, whereby I was trying to share what I learned from some very spirit-linked people in Vietnam, Djerba, Ecuador and Arizona.

"Oh yes, just as the phenomenal daughter of Geronimo said, the Body-God's Shielding Spirit can save your life, again and again, especially if you **really** believe in transcendent powers," I told Tony, hoping to increase his faith in higher levels of being.

But due to the common, [strictly material level] explanation of amazing examples of avoiding injury or death, he claimed that it was all a matter of so-called "luck."

Although the fact remains that, surely there is **no way** that people can be **taught** how to be "lucky." And yet greatly inspired by the (obviously shielded) outcome of what Tony and I just encountered, I became a thorough believer that, if ((tuned-in)) enough to the metaphysical dimension, transformative shifts into ((spiritual energy)) **can** be taught and learned.

Thus one step at a time, episode by episode, this unique book reveals the vast potentials of the injury-transcending, spirited assisted level of consciousness. All while realizing that physical-to-metaphysical transitions are a wonderful gift that God the Creator endows us with, a truly nonviolent, ((faith-empowering)) way to protect ourselves.

"And as to visible evidence of shielding energy," I said, turning to Tony. "The fact that your car is now a . . . mangled mess, but all that happened to us is . . . a couple of little nicks and bruises, well, we have just witnessed undeniable, living proof that spirit-linked salvations are not about so-called 'luck,' but about the **true** immensity of human soul-power."

"Oh yeah, you could be right about that," Tony said. "Or as Bob Marley simply puts it: 'Those who really feel it, know it' . . . Anyway, my spirit-connected friend, let's just see if we can find a path that will take us back up to the highway, okay? And then we can try to hitchhike a ride to the Marley concert, because there's probably a lot of traffic going there from Berkeley and Oakland."

And with that said and agreed with, we waved good-bye to Tony's shredded station wagon, followed by us quickly finding a narrow, somewhat meandering trail that led back up to the road.

Then, while Tony stood alongside the highway with his thumb out, I remember feeling so glad to be still alive, that I sang a verse from one of my recently recorded songs—an uplifting little ditty that goes like this:

> While nonbelievers fail to survive—
> We spiritual beings learn to **stay alive**—
> By truly activating our **Internal Sun**—
> Making soul and body become **totally one**—
> Thereby shielding ourselves from devastation—
> By evoking our ((spirit-body-emanation)) . . .

"Hey, I **really** like that one," Tony said, widely grinning. "Especially the part about the . . . Internal Sun, and how it makes soul and body totally one. Yeah man, that pretty much describes what happened to us today."

"To put it simply, yes."

Then, after about five minutes of us standing there, a woman in a red Chevrolet stopped to pick us up. And glory be, it was Gloria, the beautiful Jamaican reggae singer who, as "luck" will have it, was in Tony's band. And being that she too was on her way to that Bob Marley concert, she not only took us to that massively attended, anti-nuclear-power rally, but after it was over, she kindly drove us back to Berkeley.

Ah yes, after such an up-and-down, hellishly to heavenly day, it felt very good to be back, safe and sound in my little "birds nest," fourth floor apartment, where beaming through its front window, the full moon was brilliantly mirrored on San Francisco Bay. And although I felt a bit drained-out by the traumatic, over-the-cliff ordeal ((that was still echoing inside me)), I was very anxious to write about it in my journal, and so I transcribed several pages about the "accident" (that would stay deeply memorized in my mind).

And then, the following morning, a newly bubbling, smiling-face Tony came to my apartment for a visit, when he (quite excitedly) told me this:

"Hey brother . . . ever since yesterday, I've had this happily spiritual feeling. Oh yeah, I feel like I'm . . . brand new. And I haven't felt this way since back in 1969, when I helped to organize a huge rally . . . a gig that stopped the big University here from turning Berkeley's People's Park into a parking lot. And that was an event which made worldwide news."

And then his mood went from gleeful to sad, when he sat down and said:

"Anyway, I just found out that the agreement to let the park stay like it is has been cancelled, and now the college is again planning to make it one of their ugly, car-filled lots. And so my . . . nature-loving friend, what I came here to ask you is this: can you **please** help me organize a concert to shield our . . . icon of Keep-It-Green energy, People's Park from being destroyed?"

And so being well aware of how popular that park was, I immediately felt that Tony's plan to put together a "Keep-It-Green," musical event there was an idea to get stirred up about. "Okay sure," I said. "Let's make that . . . truly crucial rally one that will unify this whole town."

Thus began another ((protection energy)) episode, but this time it would involve what I call:

((Spirit-Linked-Protection-Energy)) Test 3: Shielding a Famously Beloved Park From Destruction

Yes indeed, mainly due to Berkeley's strong feelings about that 3-acre patch of green in its downtown area, Tony and I quickly found three popular bands who, quite anxiously, volunteered to play at our Save People's Park event. And so next came the task of putting up hundreds of posters about it.

And then came the Saturday afternoon of that ((amazingly crowded)) rally, the day after the plan to cover People's Park with cement had begun, [whereby a six-foot wide area of gray concrete had already been laid].

But a few University-hired cement-layers were surely no match for what then occurred. Because after a very uplifting band (called "Earthling Angels") gathered together a hugely park-filling audience, something very amazing happened.

To my shocked surprise, five men (all of whom wore long-flowing, green capes), walked in front of the stage while holding pick-axes, and then they proceeded to, quite boldly, smash apart the recently dried cement [that was covering a section of the grass there]. And that was a blatant action which soon caused several TV news reporters to arrive, followed by at least a dozen policemen—a helmet-wearing group who, quite obviously came to stop those men from doing their cement-breaking protest.

However, getting through that crowd to arrest those axe-wielders was no easy task, because several hundred people closely surrounded them, keeping those green-caped, concrete-busters shielded long enough to allow them to escape from the police. And from my view (on the stage), I watched them take off in their (totally green) van—all while a group of several, peace and love, Berkeley-style women kept the cops cleverly distracted, mainly by trying to hug and kiss them.

And it was then that Tony walked over to me and said:

"Hey Jess, ya know what? A reporter just told me that this rally is being televised all throughout this planet!" And duly so, because that was back when the "Green Power" movement was starting to be internationally reported—a coalition that, hopefully, will get stronger every year.

And then, while Tony and I were standing there, blissfully awed by the immensity of the crowd, Berkeley's very liberal, Afro-American mayor, "Gutsy" Gus Newport walked up to us and said:

"If it's okay with you guys, I'd like to make an important announcement."

"Okay, go for it," I told him, and after stepping up onto the stage, he said:

"Hello good people! Being that I'm mayor of this town, I just had a long talk with chancellor Adams, the man who has the last say about what happens to this . . . University owned piece of land. And due to the massive public outrage about this place becoming a parking lot, he promised me that, by tomorrow morning, the plan to do that will be **permanently canceled.** And so this park will **stay** what it is, mainly a freely open, public area, a breath of fresh air for picnics and various events. And so your beloved People's Park has been **saved. And thank you all for your justified concern!**" he hollered, echoed by a roaring cheer from at least 3,000 people.

And then, come the following Saturday, Tony and I put together another uproarious rally there, the one we titled Celebrate the Saving of Our Park—a concert aimed at congratulating the plan to (hopefully) keep that world famous location (**permanently** protected).

And to do that momentous occasion justice, along with featuring the four well known bands who, quite kindly, volunteered to play at it, I drove to Carlin, Nevada, where I persuaded the legendary Rolling Thunder to honor that event by speaking to its audience. And because his invocation was taped, I will now, word for word, quote the powerful statement that the ((aura-glowing)), Chief Thunder said to that (spellbound) crowd, all while being backed up by three of his Shoshoni drummers.

"Dear children of planet Earth, this sacred park, with its grassy field and surrounding trees and flowers, is an angel-blessed gift from the Creator. And as we have seen, due to the spiritual forces connected with Nature, when its powerful spirits get disrespected, these Creator-linked beings often fight back, sometimes with protest actions, actions that can be as mighty as what we call . . . tornados. So we should treat **ALL** Nature-linked-Spirits with due regard. And I have come all the way from my oasis in the Nevada mountains, just to personally deliver this vital message. But to add a spiritual spark to my words, I need the help of my sacred owl feather," he said. And then, as if it was a sword, he pulled a foot-long, brown and white feather (from a beaded sheaf that he wore on his belt), followed by him saying:

"Okay now, with the help of my group of tribal drummers, I will chant a song in our Shoshoni language, and while I do that, I will wave this sacred feather back and forth. And after a few lines from my song, you will see it rise into the air and dance, all by itself, because the energy of a mighty angel is within it, and that potent energy is also within **me**—a power that is silent and invisible, and yet it's as strong as the wind, and as big as the Universe."

And sure enough, while singing that mystical sounding chant, he threw that feather into the air, and after it rose a few feet above him, somehow (as if it had a life of its own), it spun around like a ballerina. And then, after it dove downward and then fluttered back up again, to everyone's stunned amazement, that ((brightly glowing)) feather flew directly **back** into Rolling Thunder's hand. And being that I was standing behind him (on the stage), I could clearly see that there were no strings (or any other gimmicks) that caused that awesome feat of magic, but only the world renown, spiritual powers that Rolling Thunder was known to possess.

Yes indeed, that ((eminently gifted)), Shoshoni wizard was the truly phenomenal summation of my (protection-energy-educated), Berkeley-based adventure.

And now that those episodes have been duly shared, our **New Era of Spiritual Consciousness Tour** now takes us to the lovely southwest coast of Mexico—a journey that, in 1983, brought about what I call:

((Metaphysical-Linked-Protection-Energy)) Test 4: The Broken Brick ((Shielding)) Test

This trip (far to the south of the Mexican border) was initially sparked by a musical project that, after several months of rounding up talented reggae musicians, I came to call Jesse Dawn and The Kind. And with the help of a (concert tour managing) friend of mine, after he set up the Kind band for performances throughout California, he then booked us to play at several clubs in Mexico's most tourist-packed city—Puerto Vallarta.

And much to our delight, our seven-piece reggae band was picked up by a big limousine at the Puerto Vallarta airport, followed by being taken to a nice hotel, where we had a splendid view of the turquoise-blue bay that highlights that amazingly scenic location.

However, after a few weeks of doing shows in some very crowded, Puerto Vallarta clubs, I encountered the ((spiritually shielded) incident that, quite possibly, could have seriously injured or killed me. And I will now describe precisely what happened during that vividly memorable night:

Okay, it was New Year's Eve, 1983, at the house where Angie (my beautiful back-up singer and girlfriend) and I rented the second floor, whereby we had much more privacy than at the hotel where, almost constantly, members of our band were visiting our room.

Anyway, just before sundown, while Angie and I were sitting in our apartment, rehearsing our duets, getting ready for the New Year's Eve crowd (at a huge club called Fernando's), we heard a man angrily shouting this:

"Hey gringo Jesse, come down here, I wanna talk to you!" he hollered, sounding obviously drunk. "I'm here in the yard, at the bottom of the stairs!"

Then, after turning on the patio light, I immediately recognized him as the very hefty, loud-talking Mexican who lived in the first floor of that house.

"Who is **that**?" Angie asked.

"It's Adolpho, the steadily drunk construction worker who lives downstairs."

"Oh, he's back from Mexico City is he? Yuk. It really bothers me the way he madly screams at his wife," Angie whispered, not wanting Adolpho to hear her.

And then, in a very garbled sounding voice, he said something about being very mad at Angie and me, because he didn't like the sound of "two gringos" singing while he was trying to watch TV.

"And if you and her don't shut up," he said, while waving a half-empty bottle of tequila in his hand. "I will come up there and kick your . . . skinny ass, Jesse. Do you comprende what I'm saying, mister big-time, Americano reggae singer?"

"Hey, que pasa, amigo, why are you so mad?" I asked him, while walking down the stairs, hoping that, if I looked him in the eyes, I could calm him down. And then, when I got within three or four yards of him, I tried to pacify his drunken anger by saying: "Hey, my friend, it's New Year's Eve, and this is **supposed** to be a night of joyful celebration."

"Oh **yeah**," he said, while bending down to pick up a brick (from the edge of the garden). "Okay then, celebrate **this!**" he shouted, while throwing that rock-hard thing directly at my face.

And when that brick hit me in the middle of my forehead, it broke into two pieces, sparking a flash of light and a sound that went **WHACK!**

And then I clearly remember just standing there, dizzily amazed that I wasn't knocked out, (along with feeling no pain at all). As suddenly I felt the urge to do some deep breaths, trying to quickly evoke an ((injury shield)), because Adolpho was coming at me with his fists up, obviously ready to fight.

And then I remembered the trick of opening my eyes **very** wide, figuring that I would try to scare him (by pretending that I was about to go **really** crazy)—a bit of mental strategy that immediately worked, because it suddenly caused Adolpho to shout:

"Eee-yah! Los Ojos del **Loco**," followed by him rapidly turning around and walking away, when he again howled that eerie "Eee-yah!" sound.

And then, while standing at the top of the stairs, Angie yelled:

"Jesse! What in the **hell** just happened? What did Adolpho throw at you? And what made him walk away **screaming** like that?"

"Who me? I never even touched him," I said. "But after he after he hit me on the forehead with a brick, I gave him a flash of what Mexicans call . . . Los Ojos del Loco. It's an old expression that, more or less means the angrily opened eyes of a crazy person, someone who might do you some . . . **serious** damage. Yeah, but what I did is not about being insanely violent, no, hardly that, I was just trying to give him a jolt of shielding energy. And as you know, that's a strongly protective emanation that, for many years now, I've been deeply exploring, along with writing a . . . work-in-progress book about it."

And then, after I walked back up to our patio, while Angie had a close look at my forehead, she said: "Wow, I can't believe it. That brick didn't even make a scratch on you. It's like you just went through . . . some kind of miracle."

"Well of course, energy forces that we don't yet really understand, we tend to call miracles," I said. "But to label spiritually evoked, protective energy as being some kind of . . . mysteriously unexplainable occurrence, **how** does that help people develop metaphysical connections?"

"Oh well, I just call it . . . good karma," Angie said. "And your good karma is connected to your spirit-body, and if your spirit-body is happy, it's connected to your love and kissing zone. So come on hon, give me a little good karma New Year's kiss, yes, give me some bliss and pucker-up those lips." And after we embraced each other, she gleefully shouted: "**Woo-hoo! Happy New Year!**"

And although I didn't feel very happy after getting hit with a brick, I then realized that being shielded from (what could have killed me) was a truly good omen, perhaps a "karmic" way to remind me that, with each new year, I was getting spiritually stronger.

And then Roberto, (the Kind's excellent guitar player) showed up in his rented van, followed by him driving us to Fernando's—the club where the trauma of that [broken brick] incident was quickly quelled, mainly by us doing what felt like our best show yet.

As again I find that, quite delightfully, there's nothing that heals the shock of a violent ordeal then some ((uplifting)), peace and love-style, positive music.

And then, lo and behold, the following afternoon, that New Year's Day became especially positive when, to our stunned surprise, Adolpho walked up to our patio, where he told Angie and I basically this:

"Hey, let me tell you people, uh . . . about last night, after I had a really bad fight with my wife, I got so drunk that I didn't even know what I was doing. And don't worry, you won't have any more trouble with me. And as for you, mister hardheaded reggae singer, the truth is, I kinda **like** your songs. So keep up the good work, amigo."

Yes indeed, Adolpho's apology was the icing on the cake of that (shocking but safeguarded) event, whereby it became another educational example of the true-to-life, ongoing potentials of ((protection energy)).

And then, two days later, after our band took its scheduled flight back to California, Angie and I soon rented a little house together, a two-bedroom place high in the hills south of Santa Cruz. And it was there that we lived in connubial bliss for over two years.

But as "fate" would have it, during our third year together, we began to have almost daily arguments—all of which led up to her leaving me, whereby she decided to move back to her home town of Los Angeles.

Thus quite sadly, I waved good-bye to one of the most vibrant love affairs that I've ever experienced.

However, being the inescapably determined author that I am, I again soothed my {lost-love} regrets by merging myself with (totally-focused), steadily undistracted book-writing.

But although the (visitors-free) atmosphere of that place kept me productively inspired, after six months of that nonstop intensity, I decided that it was again time to do some ((travel-based)) research.

And so I again returned to southeast Asia, but this time it wouldn't be to fight an unneeded war, because via this mission I would follow my **own** plan. And it was to (hopefully) interview someone who, according to worldwide reports about her, was the most (injury-shielded) person on this planet—the truly amazing woman who the Los Angeles Times called:

"The Angel-Protected President of a Nation"

After moving out of that house in the Santa Cruz hills, with the help of a check from the government (a long overdue payment given to Vietnam vets exposed to the toxic exfoliate,

Agent Orange), I launched into my first visit to the Philippine Islands.

I arrived there on September 7, 1986, eight months after the famously "shielded from murderous attacks," Cory Aquino was voted to unseat Ferdinand Marcos, the Martial Law supported, [political-opponent-killing] dictator who, quite brutally ruled the Philippines for two decades.

Thus it was no surprise that America's Time magazine named Cory "1986 Person of the Year," especially after she "miraculously" survived several Marcos regime efforts to take her life. But despite being attacked by a series of coup attempts whereby, according to worldwide reports, she was shot at "more than twenty times," she somehow avoided injury or death, all while she initiated some of the most crucially needed, humanity-helping legislation in the history of this planet.

And after checking into a very nice (but inexpensive) hotel in Manila, when I turned on the television in my room—**hello**—there President Aquino was, brightly smiling, beaming an aura so divinely luminescent, that even TV cameras clearly revealed it.

But perhaps my Philippine mission was also (divinely?) helped as well, because the second day I was there, I got hired to write a daily newspaper column, a position that soon fulfilled my plan to interview, live and in-person, the uniquely one-of-a-kind, President of a nation, Cory Aquino. However, let me tell you how that seemingly ((falling-into-my-lap)), newspaper column job came to be.

First of all, after spending my first night there in Manila, to see a bit of the splendidly beautiful, Filipino countryside, the next morning, I took a one-hour plane ride to the island of Leyte where, in a charming town called Tacloban, I checked into a small hotel. And it was there that the desk clerk told me the significant fact that, throughout the Philippines, from grades 1 to 12, all students are taught English (as a second language).

Therefore, much to my delight, my ability to communicate with Filipinos was never much of a problem.

"As you can see by looking around this town," the hotel clerk said. "Most of the stores here have English titles, names such as Amy's Grocery, or Jason's Bakery, there across street. And it's been like that ever since the 1940's, when your famous General, Douglas MacArthur liberated these islands, after the Japanese army ruled large areas here, for quite awhile."

"Wow, an Asian nation where people commonly speak English, that surely makes it a lot easier for a writer like me, especially one who wants to discover what's politically, and also spiritually, going on here." And then, after hearing me say that, the clerk handed me a leaflet that stated the following request:

"Wanted: a talented, English speaking writer to create a daily column for The Leyte Reporter, a newspaper that mixes articles written in English, together with those in the local Tagalog dialect. (Note): This publication is the most circulated one on the islands of Leyte and Samar, and has a readership of over 90,000 people. All interested applicants should go to the Editor's office at 135 Rizal Street."

Then, after realizing that this was just the kind a job I was looking for, I immediately went to that newspaper office, whereby Anthony Luzon, the kind and quite brilliant Editor of that publication, would quickly become both my good friend and boss.

"So, we now have freedom of the press again, after twenty years of Marcos trying to squash it," Editor Luzon told me, that day when I first sat in front of his desk. And then he told me about how Cory Aquino has changed all that, whereby she brought freedom of the press back to the Philippines, all while, quite bravely, she managed to survive the continuously ongoing, brutal attempts of the Marcos regime to eliminate her.

"And as many here have come to believe, it seems like there's some kind of . . . powerful angels who keep protecting her, again and again," he said, leaning back in his chair while eying me intently, keeping me beamed-in with his friendly smile.

"Yes, I also believe that good spirits watch over her," I said. "And every time I see her on TV, I immediately notice that there is a glowing aura that Mrs. Aquino radiates, a luminosity that reveals her to be someone who is . . . truly filled with light."

"Yes, my friend, you've got **that** right . . . And ya know, I think our readers would find the daily column of an American writer very interesting, especially since we're now launching a new democracy."

And then he told me that, if I wanted to write for his paper, he would sponsor me with a visa that allows me to work there for two years.

"So don't worry about that paperwork," he said. "I will take care of it. And because you come from the United States, a good ally of ours, I would like to call your daily column . . . Outside Looking In."

"Okay sir, sure, that sounds just fine to me," I said, feeling blessed for the opportunity to be a widespread, daily spokesman for Cory Aquino's history-making improvements to that country.

And then Editor Luzon reached forward to warmly shake my hand, saying: "Welcome to The Leyte Reporter."

Therefore, quite suddenly, I had a newly fervent goal—to steadily support Cory Aquino's sincere attempts to rescue the Philippines from decades of economy-destroying Martial Law, whereby she launched a truly monumental effort that the entire planet was watching.

Also, by publicly praising her efforts there, my column helped to quell the left over, traumatic guilt feelings I had about fighting a war against their closest neighbor, North Vietnam, because my role in the Philippines was happily supportive instead of [depressingly destructive].

But quite thankfully, my mind had done a 180-degree turn-around from what it was back in that Vietnamese jungle, combat zone, the place where, somehow, I dizzily sleep-walked through a year of a horror show come to life.

And yet quite unlike Vietnam, where most of its history glorifies masters of military strategy, the most honored person in the Philippines is Jose Rizal, mainly because (back in the

1890's), he wrote and self-published two books about Filipino style, peace and freedom loving philosophy. And according to an article that I read about him, there are large statues of Jose Rizal in nearly every city park in the Philippines.

Thus perhaps with the help of Editor Luzon's deep respect for a philosophic, nonviolent writer (such as Jose Rizal), after three months of transcribing my Outside Looking In column, he set me up to interview Cory Aquino, whereby my initial mission there was accomplished. And that taped (and also televised), questions and answers session went precisely like this (with Mrs. Aquino's replies in bold print):

"Dear President Aquino, after ousting Ferdinand Marcos via your overwhelming popularity, I've read reports that, along with his many failed attempts to have you murdered, he also harshly criticizes what he calls your . . . 'inexperience' in government affairs. And so please tell me, what is your response to that?"

"Well Jesse, as I recently announced at a governor's conference meeting, what Marcos calls 'experience,' is his wicked ability to have political opponents killed, all while he was massively stealing from the Philippine Treasury. And that's the kind of so-called 'experience' that we surely don't need."

"Yes indeed, you really do tell it like it is, and that's surely one of your most vital skills. And bless you for realizing how wrong it is for the president of a country to be a homicidal thief."

"But of course, knowing the clear difference between good and evil should be the primary goal of leadership. And yet, in the realm of politics, there are very few truly righteous examples to follow. However, before Marcos had him murdered, my husband, a truly good and very honest Senator, was a man totally dedicated to heartfelt representation. And without his teachings, I surely wouldn't be in the position I'm in.

"And now, fortunately for this planet, you are a new archetype of righteous change, a true-to-life healer of wrongdoings. And I'm very proud to meet the person who Time magazine, quite appropriately, named 'Person of the Year.' And so please tell me, how has that worldwide tribute affected your public image?"

"**Amazingly well. Yes, and largely due to that honor, there's been a steady stream of diplomats and media celebrities coming to visit me, kindly offering me their sincere praises for my efforts. And many of them have come from half way around this planet.**"

"So, of all the well known people who have have come to meet, greet and talk with you, who is your favorite?"

"**Oh gosh, there have been so many great ones. But I guess my favorite visitor so far is . . . India's Mother Theresa, the Nobel Prize winner who came all the way from Calcutta to tell me that I'm what she calls . . . 'a real saint.' But good heavens, I'm hardly that, I'm just a former housewife, with a persistent will to do some good things for my severely weakened country.**"

"But I can easily understand why Mother Theresa regards you so highly, especially after you've earned the reputation of being . . . shielded by guardian spirits, whereby, again and again, you have transcended the attempts of the Marcos regime to take your life."

"**Yes, apparently . . . divine intervention plays a major role in my destiny, and every day I sincerely thank my steadily life-saving, angelic spirit-guides for protecting me . . . But surely we are all spirits in the material world, if our minds are duly open to that level of consciousness.**"

"Yes, I totally agree with that. But for those who suffer from dire poverty, spirituality can be difficult to sustain. So, can you tell me some of the people-helping changes that you have already . . . put into action?"

"**Okay sure . . . Well, of course everyone deserves a decent and fairly sanitary place to live. And so I've started a nationwide program of building well-constructed apartment complexes, rent free places for homeless people,**" many of whom fell prey to the Marcos destruction of our economy . . . And also, I've initiated this country's first program to provide thousands of acres of government-owned land to struggling farmers. And surely they need that, because blessed is the hand that cultivates the land, thus providing proper nourishment for our progress-hungry nation. And along with that, I've enacted the first Presidential Commission of Good Government, a program aimed at undoing the very contagious, Marcos ploy of stealing billions from the government's treasury, money that he stashed in many secret bank accounts, secret stashes that my administration is in the process of seizing. And now, my newest project is to totally reform the Philippine's healthcare system, whereby everyone in this country, no matter what their income is, can afford to have access to truly high quality, medical services."

And then Cory stood up, and after warmly shaking my hand, she said:

"Okay then, thank you for coming here, Jesse, but I must go now because . . . in a few minutes, I will address a large group of Congress members. But please give my love to your dear Editor, Anthony Luzon, he is a truly great defender of freedom of speech, one who bravely denounced the Marcos control of news publications . . . Alright, my friend, may good spirits protect you forever, and I hope to see you again."

Then, intensely sparked by that interview, I increasingly focused my daily column on Cory's achievements and awards. For example, in January of 1987 she received the Martin Luther King Nonviolent Peace Prize, soon followed by the Eleanor Roosevelt Human Rights Award, plus the highly eminent International Prize for Freedom Award. But from my point of view, no award could compare to her unparalleled, truly historical ability to spiritually protect herself from very dangerous challenges.

And speaking of death-defying tests, in December of 1986, a few days after that interview with President Aquino, while returning to my house after a shopping trip, suddenly my **own** ((injury-shield)) was intensely challenged, whereby I encountered what I call:

((Spirit-Linked-Protection-Energy)) Test 5: The Rattletrap Motorcycle Crash Test

At that time, I was living in a small cottage on the beach, and to get to and from the newspaper office and stores, due to my meager budget, I bought a very old motorcycle. And after three months of using that relic as my transportation, apparently it was time for the inevitable breakdown to happen.

And the following description accurately recalls what, quite possibility, could have been a lethal accident:

While returning to my house on my [[somewhat shaky]] Yamaha, cruising along at about 50 miles per hour, when I tried to slow down to motivate a sharp turn to the left—(yikes)—the brake handle snapped loose and failed to work! And so unable to decrease my speed to make that turn—while the highway went to the left, I slid a few feet off its edge—unavoidably crashing (at 50 mph!) into a big tree.

But to overcome the disturbingly lingering, traumatic after-effects of a frightening ordeal, I have found that it's helpfully ((tension relieving)) to turn that experience into a piece of poetic verse.

Therefore, while truthfully describing the results of that motorcycle mishap, by writing a songlike poem about it, I can lessen its (trauma-shadows) by focusing on its positive results, doing so via a process that I call **Trauma Pacifying Poetry**—a verse of which goes like this:

> When I was forced to crash into that big tree—
> I hit it so hard that it thought it killed me—
> But all I got was a scratch below my knee—
> While the motorcycle was ruined **totally**—
> As again I **TRANSCENDED** physicality—
> By **shifting** into **SPIRITUAL ENERGY** . . .

Yes indeed, that's **really** what happened. And because that old Yamaha was so smashed-up, I left it there by the side of the road, because in the Philippines, every piece of scrap metal gets quickly recycled, and very soon someone would sell every piece of that mangled motorcycle.

Then, a few days later, as "luck" would have it, my closest neighbor, a nice fellow who worked every day in Tacloban City, kindly offered to deliver my daily column for me, thereby relieving me of the three hours it took to go to town and back on the [stopping every five minutes] bus.

And so I utilized my newly acquired free time to focus more on my column (and work-in-progress book), whereby I again merged with the WIZ (Writer's Intensity Zone) that makes "time" pass so quickly that—(poof)—days soon turned into months.

Thus those two years in the Philippines went by in a flash, whereby the visa (that allowed me to work there) expired, making it again time to move on—a transition greatly helped by a generous severance check from my Editor.

As our **New Era of Spiritualized, ((Protection Energy)) Tour** now returns to the United States, to the lovely Hawaiian Islands—where my truly **NUMBER ONE** dream—to make it **BIG** as a non-fiction author, would soon become a joyfully ongoing reality.

However, before that uplifting progression could happen, I had to again face one of my favorite challenges: trying to get comfortably situated in a place where I was a totally unknown stranger. But surely that adaptability testing, self-renewing process is one that I've become well accustomed to, especially after reading "Views From the Real World"—a very captivating book written by the wizardly, globe-trotting author, George Gurdjieff (in which he says this):

"Starting over again in a place where you're completely unknown is, by and large, a very effective way to rid yourself of any lingering ailments, all while it also greatly helps to stimulate your immunity against any kind of disease."

And yet like any beneficial skill worth learning, harnessing a new realm of experience is a procedure that requires some studious preparation. Therefore, prior to settling down into a place that I would regard as my Hawaiian "home," I explored all five of the main islands there—Oahu, Maui, Molokai, Kauai, and the one called Hawaii (also known as "The Big Island").

Then, upon discovering that The Big Island had a very active Green Party, I chose it to be the ideal location for me, mainly due to its largely unspoiled beauty—a truly special, tropical magnificence that the Green Party there has greatly helped to sustain.

And after visiting the largest town there, Hilo, where huge Banyan trees (with trunks 8 to 10-feet wide) line a street duly called Banyan Drive, I moved into a little apartment on that very green, (big-tree-dominated) street.

Thus strongly motivated by the fact that the U.S. sells more books than any other country, after two years of steadily **deeply focused** writing there, I completed the (already mentioned), 258-page book—Never "Old."

And glory be, after it was published, the immediate popularity of that book got me hired as a columnist for the ((very widely distributed)), Awareness magazine, whereby the sales of Never "Old" then took off like wildfire. But my success as an author and columnist is not what this chapter is all about, because via my (apparently inescapable) mission to experience (and thereby reveal) the vast potentials of (shielding energy), I will now accurately transcribe the truly amazing incident that I call:

((Spirit-Linked-Protection-Energy)) Test 6:
The Chevrolet Car Brake-Test

Eight years after that motorcycle mishap in the Philippines, in 1994, while living in Hawaii, I blissfully enjoyed the feeling that (hopefully), at long last, I had transcended the fate of being repeatedly challenged by life-endangering ordeals.

But as "karma" would have it, due to my increasingly evident, (spirit-linked)-revealer destiny, while on my way to spend a few hours relaxing at my favorite beach, there arose another ((shielding-energy salvation)) from what might have been a fatal accident.

However, to ease the trauma of that frightening ordeal, I will again utilize the therapeutic process of turning a shocking incident into lyrical poetry. But before I share that lyrically-rhyming, totally true-to-life poem with you, I will briefly explain the circumstances that led up to it:

Okay, it's a beautiful Sunday, and I'm feeling up-to-par in my little old Chevrolet car, cruising along at about 40 miles an hour, a normal speed for that two-lane, winding road that shoulders the coastline of northeast Hawaii.

And then, suddenly in front of me, there was a man sitting at the steering wheel of his Ford station wagon, stopped in the middle of the street, apparently stalled out. But when I stepped on my brake pedal, trying to avoid hitting that car (due to what I later learned was a leak in my brake-line), I was unable to stop!

> And then "time" uplifted into slow motion poetry—
> whereby I shifted into ((pure spirituality))—
> a force that enabled me to quickly transcend—
> a 40-miles-per-hour [[crash]] into that Ford's rear-end—
> but there was no sign of a dent on that car I hit—
> and on my Chevy, not even a scratch on it—
> plus no sign of injury on that Ford driver or me—
> and so I said a prayer of thanks to ((shielding energy))—

And then I got my car towed to an auto repair shop—
where they fixed its brakes, so it was able to stop—
And then back in my apartment on Banyan Drive—
I was still wondering (how?) I was still alive—
so I anxiously wrote about it in my journal—
sharing yet another phenomenal "miracle" . . . .

Yes indeed, although in an ((artfully)) enhanced way, that accurately explains what happened that day. Thus due to (poetically purging) myself of that hellish-to-heavenly incident, I now feel refreshingly uplifted enough to share with you my next ((injury-preventing)) event—the one that happened soon after the Chevrolet Car Brake Test.

But this experience is far more complex than being shielded from the effects of highway accidents or bullets, because it involves defending Hawaii's biggest cities from dangerously illegal passenger jets. And so I call this multi-faceted, disaster-avoiding episode:

((Spirit-Linked-Protection-Energy)) Test 7: Activating the ((Shielding Power)) of Human Rights

What initially laid out the groundwork for this crucially activated event, was my ability to buy my very first, self-owned house—a purchase made affordable by the steadily increasing sales of the Never "Old" book.

But to me, buying that very charming, five-bedroom place seemed like a ((spirit-linked)) event in itself, because it enabled me to hold seminar sessions in its splendidly seaside back yard. All of which was a new endeavor made possible by the fact that, to my stunned surprise, that house was available for the dirt-cheap (for Hawaii) price of only $100,000.

"Yep, I just put up this For Sale sign today," Andrew said, the owner of that freshly painted, amazingly affordable dwelling. And then, while I stood there, dizzily surprised that I could actually buy that sturdy and well kept, beautifully located house, Andrew said to me:

"As to why I'm selling this place for one-third of its market value, it's because I need some **very** quick cash, so I can close an important business deal, one that has to be done **today**. So if you've got the hundred thousand, this bayside, deal-of-a-lifetime is **yours**."

"Well, it just so happens that I've got that much in the bank, and I **will** go get it, because you've got yourself a buyer, my friend," I said, while gratefully shaking his hand. "And surely a five-bedroom place suits me fine, because I plan to rent the extra four bedrooms to my seminar students, people who, mainly due to the wonderful seaside view here, might want to spend a weekend at this . . . magnificent location."

And so I was soon blessed by a steady flow of people coming to my backyard classes, most of whom were readers of my Awareness magazine column—(next to which, was an ad about my seminars). And along with that, I was running televised advertisements throughout Hawaii.

But as to the next test of my ((injury-shielding)) abilities, it all began when I became angrily tired of hearing the Aloha Airlines jets that, several times a day, took-off directly over my house.

However, to counteract that continual annoyance, after discovering that most of those planes were too old to be legally in the sky, I decided to file a Rights of Protection, long-overdue lawsuit against that blatantly errant corporation.

Then, after submitting my court-action papers at the Hilo City Hall, to hear his reaction to my complaint, the next day I called the President of Aloha Airlines, over and over, until I finally got him on the phone, whereby I asked him basically this:

"Sir, why does the flight-path of your illegally old, notoriously unsafe jets continuously endanger the entire Hilo area, all while the other airlines duly avoid that take-off route? And surely you know the fact that, it's during take-offs that most planes crash, due to the enormous strain it takes to lift a big jet off the ground. And so please tell me, just **how** do you get away with using planes that, according to nationally enforced requirements, should be **banned** from the sky? Are you waiting for a jet-crashed, center-of-town disaster, before you wake-up and obey federal laws?"

"Okay, uh, whatever your name is, now listen **here**," he said, sounding obviously angered. "By taking-off over Hilo town, we eliminate five minutes of flying time, and so we save some money by using less gas, see." And then he said something about keeping his "financially struggling" airline happening, followed by him telling me this: "And if you have a beef about the way we operate, well, just go ahead and **sue** us. But I betcha our attorneys will **win** if you take that case to court!"

"Oh really, well, we will just **see** about that," I said, hanging up the phone, feeling quite glad that I filed a complaint against a company that, throughout Hawaii, was carelessly endangering not only its passengers, but everyone beneath the flight-path of their jets.

Thus being the research fanatic that I am, to back up my lawsuit, I intensely focused on gathering reported evidence about the safety record of that airlines. And just as I expected, after a day of surfing the internet, I found a long list of their violations of international safety codes.

But of all the illegal and life-threatening factors described on that list, there was one occurrence that really stood out—a very serious, faulty jet incident that, in April of 1988, killed an Aloha stewardess, along with badly injuring 68 passengers.

According to the worldwide report about that very controversial flight, it involved a "19-year old" jet that, soon after taking off from the Hilo airport, the plane suddenly lost **a big piece of its roof!** And what that terrifying situation did, was immediately vacuum a flight attendant into the sky, followed by over half of the jet's passengers being lacerated by shattered, wind-blown pieces of the aircraft's, increasingly shredding {{hole in its ceiling}}. But after some 25 minutes of that agonizing ordeal, somehow that plane was able to make emergency landing in Maui.

However, as to Aloha's extreme efforts to push its dilapidated aircraft to the breaking point, I will now quote some important information revealed by a federal probe into that roof-collapsing incident—an investigation that exposed the following report:

"The fact that the jet was nearly 20 years old was a key issue, and at the time of that tragic occurrence, it had made over 90,000 flights, far beyond the 72,000 that it was designed to sustain."

Then, after reading that significant piece of news, I called up a few local lawyers, hoping to gather some information about previously filed lawsuits against Aloha Airlines.

And according to the third attorney I spoke with, that company is run by a "very dangerous, mafia-like syndicate," whereby it's steadily being investigated for threatening the lives of whoever tries to take them to court.

And then that lawyer told me this: "What happens is, instead of paying the huge cost of buying new jets, whenever they get hit with a lawsuit, that corporation sends a couple of big thugs to the houses of whoever filed the complaint, to either bride or scare them into dropping the case."

And following that, he told me about one of his clients who, after refusing to back out of his lawsuit against that airlines, before he could appear in court, they found his body floating in Hilo Bay, killed by a bullet in his head.

"Oh yeah, that just happened a few months ago," he said. "And of course there was no proof about who murdered that guy . . . So . . . if you go ahead and take legal action against Aloha Air, be sure to watch out for some very big, dangerous-looking goons coming around to your house, wanting to have a little, so-called 'talk' with you. Do you know what I mean? And if I was you, I'd think twice about filing a case against that . . . very scary organization."

"Yeah, okay," I told him. "I'll think about it. Anyway, thanks for the info."

But due to the undeniable evidence that I had gathered, along with my strong belief in being ((spiritually protected)), I continued with the preparations for my (soon to be nationwide news), day in court.

Thus to get things rolling, after reserving a large, beachside pavilion, I hired three reggae bands to play at what I called The Save Our Skies From ILLEGAL JETS Rally, a Sunday afternoon event that, along with featuring a speech by Hilo's mayor, it was also widely televised in news reports.

Also, at that massive gathering, I gave away 500 t-shirts that had ((Save Our Skies)) printed on the front of them. And along with that, being that my lawsuit hearing was scheduled for the following morning, I handed out hundreds of flyers that urged people to come to a 9 a.m., Anti-ILLEGAL-Jets rally on the courthouse lawn.

Then, after that ((protection-energy-arousing)) event, to stir-up more support for my day in court, I did an interview at Hawaii Island's most popular radio station, K-BIG, whereby I (quite excitedly) emphasized the ((sky-saving)) importance of the demonstration at the courthouse.

But after finishing that island-wide broadcast, something very frightening happened. While I was back in my bedroom, laying down to take a break from my barrage of activities, I heard a loud knock on the front door, followed by a deep-voiced man saying:

"Hey! **Hello** in there! . . . We're from Aloha Airlines, and we want to talk to **Jesse.**"

But due to being a bit nervous about how to respond to these guys, I cautiously watched them through my (front door peephole).

And sure enough, just like that lawyer said, standing there were two men who looked like 300-pound, professional wrestlers, a pair of sunglass-wearing giants who, according to the angry look on their faces, they were not there for a friendly visit.

And then, while standing there, wondering what to do, I found myself praying for a ((spirit-linked) shield of protection.

"Hey, come on now, let us come inside," one of them said. "We want to negotiate a little deal about this . . . court case thing you got planned."

"Well, let me tell you something," I told him, while making sure the door was double-locked. "Today there was a massive anti-illegal-jets rally at Hilo's seaside park, and after seeing all that support for my case against your company, there's **no way** that I will back out of it now. And also, tomorrow morning, there's a big rally set up for the courthouse lawn, an event that will be televised news throughout Hawaii, an event that will create a huge movement against Aloha's illegal jets, a movement that **can't** be stopped."

"Oh **really**?" the man said, sounding increasingly furious. "If **that's** your attitude . . . well, don't be surprised if, before your case is heard, something **very bad** might happen to **you.** And tomorrow morning, when you get in your car, thinking that you will drive to the courthouse, it just **might blow up**. So you **better** just play it smart, and stay at home. Do you **get** what I'm saying?"

"Yeah sure, okay, I hear you," I said, hoping that he was only bluffing.

But just in case his threat was not just a scare tactic, after their (license plate removed), black sedan backed out of my driveway, I went outside and locked my car in the garage, along with making sure that its car alarm was **ON**.

As again I'm reminded of the fact that, even if the path to duly needed changes is filled with difficult challenges, it's only by taking a firm stand against corporate-level crime, that the world will become a better place.

And then, the following morning, while watching the 7 a.m., nationwide news, I discovered that the topic of unfit-to-fly, outlawed aircraft had aroused so much controversy that, even as far away as New York City, TV broadcasters were discussing my court case.

And as for those terrifying giants from Aloha Air, probably due to all of the publicity about my Rights of Protection lawsuit, I never saw them again—a ((shielding-energy)) blessing that, during my (rearview-mirror-checking) drive to the courthouse, filled me with gratitude.

Thus I made it to my lawsuit hearing feeling very "lucky," especially after being greeted by a parking lot filled with over a hundred protestors, most of whom carried signs about the danger of illegal jets. All while TV-news broadcasters roamed around, getting the opinions of various people, followed by me doing a few brief interviews.

And then, inside the crowded courtroom, I was quite glad to see a group of five people who, to my delight, not only wore the Save Our Skies t-shirts I gave them, but they also managed to secure front-row seats, where the judge could clearly see the message on their shirts.

"Hey, thanks a lot," I told them, while shaking all of their hands. "It looks like you people got here early, to get some of the best seats in the house."

"No problem," Keiko Bonk (the Green Party leader) said. "We're here to help you win this truly monumental case, because it's an issue that concerns **all** of the people in Hawaii, especially those who live near the airports."

And then the judge walked in, a stern-faced man who looked somewhat annoyed about all the noise in his courtroom, a buzz of talk that was quickly silenced when he banged his gavel, and shouted: "**Order in the court!**"

Following that, while a pair of lawyers (men in gray suits from Honolulu), tried to dispute Aloha's many violations of aviation safety laws, I kept pushing my long list of facts about their continuously illegal flights.

Then, after about an hour of hearing both sides of this important issue, the judge said that he would go to his chambers, and would return after making his decision about the outcome of this case. But when he stood up to leave the courtroom, the group wearing those Save Our Skies t-shirts, doing an apparently choreographed move, rose up from their seats and saluted him, boldly emphasizing their safety-based point of view.

And then, after only about a ten or fifteen minute wait, the judge returned, and while sitting down, he looked at me with a respectful nod, followed by him banging his gavel, and then he announced his proclamation.

But to honor what he said in news-telling, reggae-song style, I wrote a composition that I call **Salvation of the Skies**—and its first verse goes like this:

> Due to the facts that the judge was then **eying**—
> Aloha's law-breaking jets were **banned** from **flying**—
> thus only **legal** aircraft they were **ordered** to **use**—
> whereby air safety laws would stop being **abused**—
> And taking-off over cities was also a **mistake**—
> so a much safer route they were **ordered** to **take**—
> as the courtroom erupted, shouting with **glee**—
> celebrating a triumph of **POSITIVE history** . . .

And although that airline quickly obeyed the court order to permanently retire their prohibited planes, that adjustment failed to override their notoriously shoddy reputation. Therefore, unable to compete with the emergence of newer and safer airlines, Aloha soon decided to shut down their sinking-ship operation—a bit of news that surely caused a far-reaching sigh of relief—one that duly emanated throughout the Hawaiian Islands.

And speaking of long sighs of relief, what a blessing it was to no longer hear the dreadfully thundering, earth-shaking sound of jets flying over my neighborhood.

Thus mainly because of that newly tranquil atmosphere, I could again focus on what was my (long-neglected), central mission: completing a book that would go far beyond the consciousness of Never "Old."

And so for the next two years, I was deeply committed to writing what I call **The Rejuvenator's Bible**—a captivating piece of work that, after being published in 1999, delightfully launched me into new dimensions of activism.

Yes indeed, largely because of the widespread interest in that book, I became busier than ever, as not only did that volume double the size my seminars, but it also brought more attention to my Jesse Dawn and the Kind band, whereby we were getting booked throughout Hawaii.

But by January of 2002, after nearly three years of that extremely hectic, juggling-two-careers lifestyle, I decided to forego my seminars and music gigs for a while, and do a long vacation in the Philippines, mainly to rest and rejuvenate my body. Also, along with needing a break from being constantly in demand, I decided it was time to take a ((soothing separation)) from the presidency of "Bad Brain" Bush, because I was thoroughly tired of hearing about what I call his Oil Wars Incorporated.

And then, after two months in a Filipino beach house, where I gladly avoided any news about the blanket-bombing of Iraq, I returned to the U.S., very ready to record my newly written, anti-war songs—soon to be released on a CD that I titled **A Peaceful Culture.**

But as to the (injury transcending) dimension that this chapter aims to uniquely explore, the following episode is one that took me to seemingly uncharted levels of ((spiritual-level guardianship)), mainly by experiencing what I've come to call:

((Spirit-Linked-Protection-Energy)) Test 8: The Phenomenally ((Injury-Shielding)) Birth of Jahson Event

However, before we get to the part of this chapter that the title (above) represents, let me tell you the circumstances that led up to that episode, whereby (protection energy), to a large extent, evokes its most ((life-saving)) dimension.

First of all, I should emphasize that, during the summer of 2006, while in Hawaii, I decided to (totally dedicate) myself to the task of completing what is clearly my most conscious book—the long-labored volume that is now ((hopefully)) coming to life in **YOUR** hands.

But despite my fervent efforts to put this extremely self-empowering, literary journey together, mainly because of the steady flow of people coming to my house (mostly seminar guests, neighbors and musicians), at that time, writing this book there was impossible.

And so it became quite evident that, in order to ((effectively)) transcribe the multifaceted potentials of what I call The New Era of Consciousness, I needed to find a relatively undistracted, visitors-free place to write.

Then, after thinking about where to go to find the needed solitude, what kept coming to mind was the serene tranquility I found in the Philippines, where a nicely secluded, seaside house can be rented for an amazingly small price. And so back to that peaceful piece of tropical paradise I went.

As our **New Era of Spiritualized, Mind-Over-Body Tour** now returns to a splendidly unspoiled part of the Philippines, where I discovered a truly gorgeous, north coast place called Pasaleng Bay.

And it was there that I rented a cement-walled, nicely furnished house on the beach, a very secluded dwelling that, to my surprise, was available for only seventy-five dollars a month.

However, although Pasaleng seemed like the perfect place to write this book, it would eventually become the most frightening testing-ground of my ((spirit-linked)) abilities.

And yet, while blissfully unaware of the monumental challenges that I would encounter there, the magnificent beauty of that area inspired me to write a little song about it—a lyrical piece that I call **Pasaleng You Make My Writing Sing.** And the first verse of it goes like this:

Here in this utopia by the **sea**—
I have found some pure **serenity**—
calmly nestled amid this tropical **grace**—
the peacefulness here is easy to **embrace**—
greatly helping me to do what I **should**—
a literary work that is ((**timelessly**)) **good** . . .

And speaking of timelessness, after seeing the pristinely untouched, ancient rainforest that shouldered Pasaleng Bay, I came to realize how vastly different that place is from seaside locations in Hawaii, where nearly all of its coastline has been deforested by nonstop development. All of which has sky-rocketed the price of beachfront land there, a situation that has caused Hawaii's super-rich, State government to be the main buyer of it, whereby they make huge profits by renting it (by the square-foot) to hotels, restaurants, night clubs and homeowners. And that is why my half-acre lot in Hawaii was not mine but, quite expensively, leased to me by the State. And so the only thing (at that location) I could afford to own is the house.

But in Pasaleng, after realizing that I could buy ocean-side land there for a tiny fraction of its cost in Hawaii, I bought five acres of it—a piece of God's creation so filled with huge trees and flowers that, when I walked into the depths of its forest, I could hardly believe my eyes.

And then, after discovering that a part of those precious acres was a treeless field (with a drinkable mountainside spring next to it), I realized that it was an ideal spot to have a vacation home built—a place to fulfill my dream of living in a pristine garden of Eden.

And with that plan in mind, I hired a contractor (along with his crew of a dozen construction workers) to make a thick-walled, cement structure that mirrored my drawings of it. Thus for a total cost of about $40,000, that hard-working group took five months to make my self-designed, curvilinear shaped dwelling—a rather unique place (nicely painted in many shades of green), with a third floor patio that overlooks spectacular Pasaleng Bay.

And as a final touch to this palace-like building, I decorated its gently curving front wall with its ((rainbow-colored)) name, dubbing it Zion House.

As I then discovered the continually ongoing, deep satisfaction of designing the shape (and interior layout) of my own, pride and joy house, a creation that, in many soothing ways, echoes the gentle curves of the ancient rainforest surrounding it.

However, I do admit that, after a few months of living there, steadily writing (while getting more and more attached to the top floor room that I call my Ziontific Zone), it got to be, as they say, "lonely at the top."

But I soon came to realize that so-called "loneliness" was, quite crucially, what was needed to create this increasingly beyond the "norm," ((multi-dimensional)) book, especially the parts that evolve [relatively unexplored] levels of consciousness.

Although finally, in the summer of 2008, my self-induced cocoon of solitude was blissfully ended, because I then met the very well educated (and also very lovely), Lanie-Rose, a Filipina who, to my delight, speaks perfect English. And largely due to our ability to easily communicate, we have maintained a very compatible, steadily flowing relationship, especially after realizing the truly **big** difference between simply basic, physical lust and **true** love.

Thus after happily living together in Zion House for over a year, via the sweet passion that developed between us, Lanie Rose gave birth to our beautiful baby boy, a half-Filipino/half-American "mestizo" who we named Jahson.

And yet, as my (ever teaching me) fate will have it, on October 24, 2009, the day that child was born, I experienced a (protection-energy) test that goes far beyond the ((spiritual dimension)) of any episode previously transcribed in this book.

But let me tell you the circumstances that led up to that extraordinary, truly momentous encounter, one that involves Nature's most widely powerful force—the energy of wind and rain.

First of all, I should explain that, when I initially decided to have a house built in Pasaleng, no one told me how frequently hurricanes come to that north coast region. But ever since my first winter there (in 2006), when I became very focused on tracking typhoons with my computer, I discovered that, year after year, from August through December, that part of the Philippines gets hit by some of most dangerous cyclones on Earth.

And it was during that ominous October of 2009, when no less than three "Super" typhoons (those which generate 150+ miles-per-hour winds) came very close to directly hitting the Pasaleng area—all within the same month. First came Super Typhoon "Choi-wan," a cyclone that, about 50 miles to the east of Zion House, caused severe flooding and landslides, while it also took the lives of 24 residents of that northeast coast location. And then, a week later, came Super Typhoon "Parma"—a hurricane that totally devastated nearly the same area that "Choi-wan" did, whereby the combination of those two storms destroyed over 800 homes, along with killing a total of 112 people. But like so many of the typhoons that I've tracked on my computer, although "Choi-wan" and "Parma" were headed directly for Pasaleng, for what I see as ((spirit-linked)) reasons, that pristine region was, again and again, shielded from getting major hurricane damage.

And then, on October 23rd (the day before Jahson was born), yet another massive typhoon was steadily approaching the Zion House area—the cyclone called Super Typhoon "Lupit." But this time, quite shockingly, that storm was energizing wind speeds of over 165 miles per hour, a velocity that made it one of the most potentially lethal hurricanes in the history of the Philippines.

Then, come the morning of October 24th, while the (outer edge) of Super "Lupit" was barraging Pasaleng with intense winds and rain, Lanie Rose (who was then visiting her parents in a nearby town) called me on her cell phone, to excitedly tell me this:

"My mother says that, due to my labor pains, our baby son will probably be born in a few hours. And so right now, we are at the Laoag Provincial Hospital, in the maternity ward. So **please** come here as soon as you can. And I hope and pray that you can get here before this . . . Typhoon Lupit floods the roads, and makes getting here . . . nearly impossible."

"Okay, don't worry honey, just try to stay calm," I said. "I will jump into my jeep right now, and I **will** get there . . . no matter what."

As I will now describe what I call Jahson's Birthday Miracle, a truly extraordinary, surely ((shielded by angels)) experience that went precisely like this:

When I arrived at that hospital, being that it was at the southern edge of Super Typhoon "Lupit," there was already about six inches of rain (on the street in front of its parking lot). And then, upon entering the maternity ward waiting room, when I told a nurse why I was there, after she looked out a window, nervously eyeing the heavy downpour outside, she turned to me and said:

"Well sir, right now, Lanie Rose is going through the process of giving birth to your child, so please have a seat, and just wait here, because visitors are not allowed in the ward where babies are delivered."

And so I sat down, and then anxiously pulled my laptop computer out of its leather case, hoping to see a change in Super Lupit's direction. But at that time, the report I (tuned-into) was extremely frightening. Because according to the typhoon-tracking website (that I've found to be very accurate), that cyclone's 165 miles-per-hour hour winds would soon devastate the entire northwest coast of that island, a region that included not only that hospital, but also precious Pasaleng Bay and Zion House.

Therefore, just like I did with all of the other (directly approaching) hurricanes, I intensely (inner voiced) prayers to the Sky Spirits—the truly **good** angels who, so many times before, had protected that area from being seriously damaged by typhoons.

And then, after a nurse turned on the TV in that waiting room, she said: "This is a local broadcast . . . it's coming from the biggest church in this town."

As suddenly I was drawn into watching a televised event that was truly memorable. It was a congregation of about 500 people, all of whom were being led in prayer by a minister wearing a (green robe)—a kindly looking man who told his packed-in, (church-filling) audience basically this:

"Yes, my children of Sacred Creation, I am very glad that so many of us here, quite steadily believe that this part of the Philippines is linked to what the Bible calls . . . The Garden of Eden. And thankfully, ever since I've been living in this area, I've seen that our prayers to preserve the beauty of this north coast province **really** work! And now, when our faith is **so crucial**, we must realize that the **real,** so-called 'superpower' is . . . kindness and mercy, yes, as we again earnestly pray for spiritual protection from this hopefully quelled . . . Typhoon Lupit."

Then, after hearing that, because I had seen at least a dozen hurricanes somehow, some way, get steered away from that very special region, I became another one who truly believes that a Garden of Eden-like, beautiful area is a (sacredly shielded) zone. And so along with that north coast style, ((deeply united)) group of people in that church, I totally merged with the message of their prayers.

And then, after hearing that congregation's very emotional, heartfelt singing about their faith in (Nature-shielding and people-saving angels), I again focused on the screen of my computer. When suddenly I could hardly believe what I was seeing, because before my eyes, there was a hurricane-tracking statement so amazing that, to save it for posterity, I immediately copied it into my computer's Documents section. Therefore, word for word, I will now share what that truly unforgettable, ((prayer-answering)), website report said:

"Category 5, Super Typhoon Lupit has totally reversed its direction, whereby it's made (a somewhat miraculous), 180-degree U-turn. And it is now, quite unexplainably, moving back into the South China Sea, where it probably won't do any serious damage."

"Hello mighty north coast saviors in the sky!" I shouted (while looking through a window), where lo and behold, the rain and wind had stopped, as suddenly the horizon had turned clearly blue, and a double-((((rainbow)))) appeared—an Omen of Strong Faith indeed.

And then, as if on cue, a nurse came walking up to me and said:

"Sir, a few minutes ago, your very healthy, beautiful baby son was born. So come, follow me, and I will show where he and his mother are resting."

"Okay sure, lead the way," I told her, feeling somewhat dizzied by the salvation that I just witnessed. And then, after being led to where Lanie held our (delightful to behold), baby son, she said to me:

"Jesse . . . would you like to be the one to name him?"

"Well . . . if you want me to grant me that honor, considering the spirit-linked, typhoon turn-around that coincided with his birth, if it's okay with you, I would like to give him a name that connects with who the reggae culture calls Jah, The Spirit of Merciful Nature. And so I would like to call him . . . Jahson."

And then, after a few seconds of deliberation, while lighting up her lovely face with a smile, Lanie Rose said:

"Hmm, Jahson, well . . . okay, I think I like the sound of that . . . Yes, that name will always remind us of this very miraculous, super typhoon avoiding day. Wow, what a blessing, everybody in his ward is talking about how that . . . amazingly powerful storm did a **total** turn-around."

And it surely did.

But, still I wonder how weather experts justify the supposedly "mindless" forces that can quickly alter the course of hurricanes, whereby "scientific" reasoning habitually ignores the ((upper-half)) of reality—the realm of the spiritual world dimension.

However, I'm sure that [strictly material-based] reasoning will eventually realize that, along with pollution-caused, global-warming, all hurricanes are strongly influenced by the Creator designed, pristine beauty of Nature, whereby divine creation is duly protected.

Protected indeed, as I increasingly realize the fact that, the more humanity evolves beyond [spooky-ghost] clichés, and thereby connects to the ((spirit-linked emanations)) that are both (within) and steadily watching over us, the more we will activate:

The TRULY MIGHTY Power of Prayer

Yes indeed, as we have (hopefully) seen via this book, my exploration into prayer-induced, (protection energy) keeps going on and on, all of which is based on true-to-life, personal experiences.

And as to the origin of my strong belief in (rainstorm quelling) prayers, it began back in 1994, when I organized the first of my annual Bob Marley Day festivals in Hawaii, an event to honor the February 6 birthday of that truly legendary singer-songwriter.

Surely it was that occasion which taught me that, to make all twelve of those free-of-charge, outdoor concerts gather the huge crowds that they did, being that East Hawaii (from November through February) is one of the rainiest places on Earth, it required **lots** of praying for sunshine.

And glory be, every time that I hosted that early February festival, although the usual, heavy downpour of wintertime rain kept falling, at the beginning of each of those gatherings, suddenly the sun came out and **STAYED** out, all the way through **all twelve** of those events!

However, the amazingly sudden weather changes (that saved those festivals) were, as I see it, mainly due to the prayers of the massive amount of Bob Marley Day fans—together with the truly monumental power of Marley's spirit. And as to publicized evidence of his enormity, during his (physical level) life here on Earth, Marley wrote so many highly conscious, ((prayer-like)) songs that, in 1999, America's Time Magazine chose his "Exodus" album to be honored as "The Greatest Album of the 20th Century."

Also, in regard to the ((spirit-linked-shielding)) abilities of he who became well known as "Natural Mystic" Marley, consider the facts of what happened to him on December 3rd, 1976—an incident that made worldwide news:

According to the Wikipedia.org, internet encyclopedia, at about 7 p.m. on that December night, Bob Marley was attacked by a gunman who, while standing just a few feet away from him, shot him with a bullet that penetrated the area directly in front of his heart. But what that 45 caliber bullet did (after causing just a shallow wound), was bounce off his chest and then lodge itself into Marley's left forearm. And then, after discovering that he was shot by a hired killer (a man paid to stop him from performing at the "Smile Jamaica" concert)—an event organized by Jamaica's Prime Minister—Bob Marley then did something that duly maximized his global popularity. And that was this:

Just two days after getting gunshot wounds in his chest and arm, to overcome the ploy to stop him from performing at that concert, a ((prayer-healed, bullet-defying)) Marley went ahead and did a very lively, 90-minute set there. All while over 80,000 fans uproariously cheered, fervently honoring him like he was an invincible angel from God.

Oh yes, as we have repeatedly seen, ((**invincibility**)) **is the KEY to REAL success.**

And when it comes to his role among the "stars" of music, I believe that no one yet has equaled Bob Marley's ability to see, write and sing about the spiritual side of things—a wondrously creative skill that calls to mind these words from the writings of Mahatma Gandhi:

"Amid the darkest of skies, the brightest stars stand
out, continually revealing their luminous creativity."

Thus in regard to the vastly beneficial effects of what
Gandhi called "luminous creativity," that is the central topic
of the next chapter of this book. And so again I say, read on
dear reader, read on, and never lose your faith in the truly
((universal)) powers of creation over destruction . . .

(((CHAPTER FIVE)))

THE ((SELF-RENEWING ENERGY)) OF CREATIVITY

"Every artist dips a paintbrush into their soul, and then
therapeutically depicts what is seen there."
—Henry Ward Beecher

"Once you discover the healing powers of your personally
created mind, you should steadily give yourself to it."
—Buddha

Good advice indeed, as the great Buddha was surely one of the
rare people who, quite indelibly, spread the timelessly creative
art of ((spiritual word-power)). And now that we're focused on
perpetually artful proclamations, I duly recall this one from the
world-famous journal of Michelangelo, the extraordinary artist
who, at the age of 88, wrote this potent statement:

"I grow more intensely creative every year." Thus he
transcribed a declaration that, if thought about, brings to
mind this significant question:

HOW IS CREATIVITY REJUVENATING?

At the very roots of the creative process, there dwells the reality that the original life-forms on Earth were plants, steadily evolving organisms initially brought into being by ((sunlight merging with water))—a fact that unfolds this delightful realization: Planet's Earth's original spark of creativity was a sunbeam.

However, depending on the roots of our beliefs, there are many fascinating theories about what activated the creation of life on Earth. For example, while in Australia, where I spent several weeks studying the Aborigines theories of what they call The Re-Birthing-Dreamtime Mind, the 107 year-old, chief of an ancient tribe there told me that, for many thousands of years, their motto continues to be this:

> "All of life begins with **SINGING** it into creation."
> And to verify that concept, I recall him pointing out the
> fact that, every time a human baby is born, amid his or
> her exit from the womb, the infant unfurls a wailing,
> aboriginal-style chant of newborn arrival.

And speaking of the songs of newly born arrivals, whenever I walk through my garden, I hear the birds chirping sweet-sounding gratitude to the berry bushes and papaya trees, and so I join in with them, gleefully humming a tune. But to me, this urge involves much more than just uttering musical sounds, because I know that melodic vocalizing oxygenates brain cells, and thereby activates immunoglobulin, an important secretion that strengthens our immunity and healing systems. And so maybe a song a day DOES keep the doctor away, which is why I highly recommend daily sessions of tuning-up your vocal chords, perhaps simply done by chiming in with a song on your stereo, (which is also a good way to cheer yourself up).

All while realizing that singing is much more than just a fun thing to do at birthday parties.

Ah yes, the good "old" birthday celebration. But of course, via the scientifically **proven**, inborn ability to perpetually renew every cell of our bodies, even while sleeping, we **STAY** busily re-creating ourselves, willfully sparking-up the ((ongoing)) process of physical renewal. Therefore, I will now wish all of my readers a **HAPPY EVERYDAY RE-BIRTHDAY!** And along with that, due to realizing the ((ceaselessly regenerating)) ability of this precious planet, let me also wish you all **HAPPY EVERYDAY BE-EARTH-DAY!**

But as to the notion of being labeled by a [numerical] perception of one's age, it all comes down to the annual, so-called "birthday" being perceived in one of two ways: we can either be a **D.O.W.N.**, a [**D**umped **O**n **W**ith **N**umbers] victim, or an **U.P.**, a creatively **U**nnumbered **P**erson. And as **U**nnumbered **P**eople, perhaps we can have a better understanding of why little children are so frequently joyful, mainly because their numerical "age" means nothing to them, and so they have no reason to [worry] about its effects on their bodies.

And by watching my 2 year-"old," (bundle-of-creativity) son, I've noticed that, like most infants, he gleefully enjoys picking up various objects, followed by combining them into a primitive creation that, to his eyes, is a work of art, even if it's just a bottle cap wrapped in some paper.

Also, along with that, even in infancy, he has a lively appreciation of rhythmical music, an inherent urge whereby he not only ((sings along)) with songs on the stereo, but he also waves his arms in the air, dancing along with his singing.

Yes, regardless of how "old" we are (or think we are), by activating the creativity within us, we effectively quell our spells of mental depression, all while realizing that mind-over-body wellness is not about the years in our life, but **the life in our years**.

And in regard to examples of very creative people who, quite famously, lived very long, steadily artistic lives, let's take a closer look at:

The Effects of Making Art on the Aging Process

To support the fact that creativity sparks self-renewal, consider the longevity of famous artists such as Pablo Picasso, Georgia O'Keeffe, Willem de Kooning and Marc Chagall, all of whom painted well into their 90's, Chagall still doing it at 97, and O'Keeffe still steadily painting at 98.

And how can we omit the amazing Grandma Moses, a woman who, at the age of 81, put together the first exhibition of her paintings, and from there on her fame skyrocketed, whereby at the age of 101, she had become the most well known American artist of all time. And even when she had lived more than a century, she still appeared at all of the exhibitions of her paintings, events that drew thousands of people, as far and wide, they came to see not only her charming works of art, but also her stunningly ageless vitality.

However, it's important to realize that, not only famous artists evoke the important link between creativity and longevity, but that connection also prevails throughout every strata of society.

For example, there is my wife's grandmother, Sixta, a blissfully sweet Filipina who, even at the age of 109, she manages to stay steadily creative, busily weaving various kinds of hats (made from palm tree leaves), most of which she hand-paints with colorful designs. And without fail, every day of the week, Sixta not only sells her handmade creations at outdoor markets, but to attract the attention of customers, she also sings about them, chanting little verses that go something like this:

157

"My hats last a **very** long time, while they shade you from the **hot** sunshine, and when it rains, they **keep** you dry, so come look at my **hats**, and please **don't** pass me by!"

Thus by combining her weaving and painting with daily singing sessions, she has developed what she calls "Sixta's System of Vibrant Longevity." And although the [Old Era], strictly drugs and surgery-based medical industry would probably call Sixta's System "unscientific," I believe that, due to the amazingly good condition she is in, at 109, she is **truly** a champion in the field of sustained vitality.

And as to her effect on me, mainly due to witnessing her steadily blissful creativity, I continue my urge to paint (and also photograph) landscapes, especially in the springtime, whereby the Pasaleng area is gloriously abloom with new flowers and freshly green leaves on the trees. Yes indeed, even in the tropics, the months of April and May are splendid examples of Nature's perpetual renewal. And after seeing the amazingly colorful, springtime effects that surround Zion House, I took a picture of that gorgeous scene, a photo that was soon echoed by painting a large mural of it, one that spread across the third floor, bedroom wall. And to give that painting a spark of spirituality, I included the radiant rays of ((protection-energy)) that, to my eyes, steadily shield that precious area from typhoons.

Also, following that, I did a second mural that brightened up the kitchen, again enhancing the Zion House location with (protector-spirit) emanations.

Then, next to the kitchen wall mural, to clarify its message, I taped a copy of a little verse I wrote, a lyrical piece of thankfulness that says this:

When springtime brings its vast array of flowers,
new creation reveals its ((ceaseless)) powers,
re-creating the leaves stripped by winter's winds,
as the season of rebirth superbly begins,

and when angry typhoons bring their agitation,
Nature's gift of beauty blesses us with protection . . .

As I again inhale my love of the natural world and exhale gratitude, easing my [inner-tension] with a steady belief in the Creator's grand design, whereby a newly blooming tree urges us to say "Ahh."

Oh yes, the beauty of Earth steadily creates peace of mind, especially for those who learn to feel its soothingly therapeutic influence.

Therefore, due to its pacifying effects, perhaps making paintings that echo photos of splendid scenery should be a required part of the personal agenda of politicians, whereby their constant support of warfare could, quite possibly, be quelled by the process of ((creation)) versus [[destruction]].

Or as the singer, song-writer and peace activist John Lennon wisely put it:

> "To prevent undue wars, peacefully creative people should, quite urgently, move from the ivory tower to the **CONTROL TOWER** of society, because lovers of God's beauty are those who **should** rule countries."

And he speaks the truth, because creative minds have **always** been the initiator of the peacemaking progress. For example, the internationally known poet, painter and peace activist, Walt Whitman, greatly helped President Lincoln with the wording of The Emancipation Proclamation, the classic document that negotiated an end to America's (1861-1865), very bloody Civil War.

However, Whitman's style of diplomacy was not politically oriented, but deeply guided by his conscience—a ((poetically visionary)) way of thinking that made him widely known as "The Great Exemplar of Spiritual Goodness Within."

And surely the study of soulful goodness is sorely needed amid this war-weary world, where we are steadily programmed to believe that "ignorance is bliss," all while stupidity continues to be a major cause of destructive violence.

But to achieve a new era of peacefully creative consciousness, various educational approaches need to be utilized, methods that are not only philosophical, art-making and spirit-connected, but also musical, and even occasionally humorous.

Or as the delightfully artful (and often sarcastic) writer, Mark Twain said in one of his articles:

> "Although living on planet Earth is quite expensive, it does include an annual free trip around the sun. So if and when you have the time, try to relax, stay calm, and ENJOY the journey."

And then Twain's creatively witty, "enjoying the journey" type of reasoning went on to transcribe this:

> "I have found that to happily succeed in life, we need three things: A wishbone, a backbone, and a funny bone."

And then he jokingly asks us this question: "How long is a minute? Well, it depends on which side of the bathroom door you're on."

And then Twain follows that by getting more seriously poetic, when he helpfully lets us know that:

> "Hate does more harm to the vessel where it's stored, then to anyone on which it is poured, but if we can sustain a creative spirit, we will learn how to peacefully steer it."

And hopefully, by ((internalizing) that message, humanity will come closer to perceiving the creatively healing, truly life-saving effects of what has come to regarded as "inner-spirit."

But what **IS** is inner-spirit, and how can we **clearly** define it? Well, according to Webster's New World Dictionary, the word "spirit" is defined as something so uplifting that it deserves to be repeated in bold type and capital letters:

"SPIRIT: AN ANIMATING FORCE HELD TO PROVIDE LIFE TO PHYSICAL ORGANISMS"

Take note here that "spirit" animates life by being **HELD** onto, a description that points to the significant fact that, more than anything else, ongoing well being is a struggle to **NOT LET GO** of ((perpetually re-creating)) spirituality.

But to effectively activate the regenerating powers ((within us)), an initial step is to overcome the fear of being an individual, because it's mainly outstanding individuals whose lives are greatly honored, especially when they are a source of truly beneficial philosophy. And yet, in regard to the totalitarian programming that, again and again, tries to make people afraid of being an "abnormal" individual, I recall the words of the great American poet and teacher, Ralph Waldo Emerson, when he memorably unfurled the following piece of wisdom:

> "One of the most important truisms of all is this: people who are not steadily conquering their fears of being an ever-learning, mind-expanding individual, have not yet realized the most precious secrets of life."

And of course, it's the ((transcendently)) unique people who, century after century, continue to be the worshipped deities of various religions.

However, despite the numerous differences that separate one religious doctrine from another, basically, they all have one central theme in common: the belief that so-called "death" is somehow followed by an "afterlife"—be it "heaven" or "Holy Zion" or "reincarnation." All of which points to what is seen as this crucial fact of life:

Self-Creating, Spiritual-Energy Never TOTALLY Dies

As I think about the vast amount of possibilities of living a ((perpetually re-created existence)), I am reminded of when my father passed on, back in April of 1997, when he was 86. At his funeral, I was quite saddened to hear the continuously repeated, supposedly "appropriate" phrase of "may he rest in peace"—a saying that relegates us a totally uncreative, spirit-deadened, "Final Resting Place."

But as to the "rest in peace" (R.I.P.) notion, it completely defies the unending cycles that rule this planet, whereby both the sun and moon "disappear," only to ceaselessly rise again. And as I steadily emphasize, spring **always** follows winter, whereby (apparently) dead trees and flowers, ((quite naturally)) come back to life—a fact that, again and again, is clearly undeniable.

Thus by becoming a firm believer in the true-to-reality, steadily enduring power of natural creation, people can duly TRANSCEND the "standard" R.I.P ["Rest in Peace"] notion, whereby the letters R.I.P. should, quite faithfully, stand for **R**ebirth **I**s **P**erpetual.

Or as Pablo Picasso artfully put it:

> "As to the ongoing rebirth called reincarnation, it's deeply understood only by those who, quite clearly realize that re-creating oneself is the very opposite of self-destruction, whereby a permanent death is *not* desired."

But unfortunately, the path to [dead-end finality] gets steadily promoted by the massive amounts of murder and misery featured on TV—the constantly brain-numbing, [self-destructive] programming that **surely** needs to be alleviated.

And so again I ask, instead of emphasizing people's wondrously self-renewing skills of creativity, **WHY** does the media steadily bombard us with [brain-depressing], nauseating scenes that glorify the brutality of war? Can it be some sort of covert conspiracy to depopulate an overcrowded Earth, whereby we become so intensely paranoid that, by jumping to [misguided conclusions], we will die an early death?

However, as for my ((hopefully)) evolving, **Waking Up to the REAL Me life,** I try to encourage peacefully human progress by writing books, magazine articles and songs about the realities of creatively healing energy. And it's via that uplifting ((frame of mind)) that I wrote the following verse, part of a recently recorded song that I call:

Real Creativity Chooses Peace

Surely **everyone** is creative, regardless of age or "race"—
And to re-create **ourselves** is truly a saving grace—
And as for **my** "race," I'm part of the **HUMAN Family**—
A realm that helps me increase the peace by creating
   UNITY—
Yes, creativity IS The Source, whereby we live **perpetually**—
The energy that makes one's (inner-soul) able to live
   eternally—
But the **ultimate** creation is of course **HAPPINESS**—
wherein we find **peace of mind** that duly keeps us
   BLESSED . . . .

(((CHAPTER SIX)))

((PROTECTION ENERGY))
vs.
MEDICAL MISTAKES

"Even when they are difficult to believe, helpfully beneficial facts can often save your life."
—Benjamin Franklin

Thus by realizing the truth of Mr. Franklin's statement, our most effective defense against medical procedure errors is, first of all, learning about how and why they happen. However, not only are the mistakes involved with conventional medical practices alarmingly on the rise, but so are the prices being charged for them, whereby healthcare is riding a sky-rocketing inflation rate of **20 percent** a year. And that runaway rocket just keeps on flying higher, steadily battling against government regulation of doctor's fees and pharmaceutical prices. But of course, when a disease or injury is threatening your life, if you're rich enough, money is no object, all while it's a serious, panic-causing crisis for people of middle and lower class incomes.

Thus being ((educated)) about [habitually overlooked], increasingly problematic aspects of the medical industry has become **vitally** important, especially when it involves:

Frequently Inaccurate Medical Tests

According to a very informative book called "Medicine On Trial," upon getting a medical "check-up," the routine number of tests given to a (potential patient) is fifteen or more. But studies revealed in "Medicine on Trial" say that these tests are only **"65 percent accurate,"** and so even if someone is quite healthy, they have **"one chance in three of being subjected to totally unneeded treatments."**

Salesmen call this profit-making technique "creating a customer."

But to protect yourself from an incorrect diagnosis, try to keep in mind that it's only **ONE doctor's point of view**, a notion that, without fail, should be backed up by another physician's **EVER CRUCIAL second opinion.**

However, situations often arise whereby, getting a second opinion is not a doable option, especially when it comes to the most commonly overdone surgery of all, the continually on-the-rise:

Unnecessary Cesareans

According to well documented statistics, since 2008, the frequency of cesarean operations has **doubled**, whereby in many countries (especially in the U.S.) they have come to account for nearly **25 percent** of baby deliveries.

And as to why there is a steadily increasing amount of surgery-induced births, extensive research reveals this rather disturbing fact:

More often than ever before, these operations are done as a convenience for baby-delivering doctors, whereby they don't have to be up all night, waiting around for a normal delivery. And along with that, cesarean surgery not only quickens the birthing process, it also quadruples the physician's fee.

But of course, not all doctors are impatient greed-heads, and yet unfortunately, many of them are. And so we should be ever on the alert for those who just want to cut and run, especially if we realize that most of these practitioners operate within a system that, more and more, lacks the oversight needed to keep them properly under control.

Yet another overdone surgical procedure is the one that, according a vast amount of research, involves what has come to be:

An Increased Frequency of Unneeded Mastectomies

As most of us now realize, the breast removal operation called "mastectomies" has become a habitually "standard" treatment for breast cancer—a disease that, in the United States, now causes over 40,000 fatalities a year.

And as to why this form of cancer has become so epidemic, according to a very revealing book called "Dressed to Kill," the authors, medical researchers, Sydney Singer and Soma Grismaijer, after studying over 4,500 women (in five cities across the U.S.) duly expose this startling information:

"Because of the suppression of (vital to the body's immunity system) lymphocyte circulation, THREE OUT OF FOUR WOMEN who, quite repeatedly, wore their bras 24 hours a day, eventually developed breast cancer."

All of which is a dilemma linked to what is becoming a well known fact:

The main circulator of ((bloodstream-cleansing)) lymphocytes are lymph nodes, vital organs located at the outer edges of the breasts: the very same place where [tight-fitting] bras steadily block ((lymphocyte circulation)).

As I again refer to the (perhaps life-saving) book "Dressed to Kill," in which the following, quite significant statistics are revealed:

"1 out of 7 women who wore bras 10 to 12 hours a day developed breast cancer. But among the women who wore their bras 5 to 6 hours a day, only 1 out 152 of them got breast cancer."

Therefore, due to the truth of these well researched facts, all of you brassiere-wearing women out there, **PLEASE** ((protect yourselves)) from lymph-node obstruction, simply by regularly loosening your bra (or taking it off when at home, where there's probably no need wear it).

Thus hopefully, more and more people are realizing the importance of what the [Old Era] medical industry calls the "**P**-word"—**PREVENTION**—the irreplaceable ((shielding-energy)) factor that, quite clearly, should be a crucial part of **everyone's** education.

As we now move on to another piece of vitally important information, a report recently uncovered by the New York Times. And I will duly quote from this rather shocking article titled:

"Heart Bypass Surgery Linked to Brain Damage"

"Major studies have found that heart bypass surgery causes continually lingering, brain impairment in a surprisingly high number of patients—nearly 25,000 a year. The ongoing brain malfunction occurs when the machine that circulates the patient's blood (during the bypass operation), quite often dislodges blood clots that, according to recent studies, steadily impair the cerebral portion of the mind, mainly by reducing its oxygen supply."

The Times article then goes on to say that the brain injury caused by this procedure often causes "strokes, seizures, and a pronounced deterioration in concentration and memory."

"Oh well," the medical industry moguls might say. "The sometimes bad side-effects of surgery are, in fact, just a part of the cost of survival, are they not?"

Ah yes, the good old "cost of survival" code of "medical justice"—the same so-called "justice" uncovered by this September, 2011, worldwide circulated, internet report, a rather mind-jolting bit of news that reveals the following (quoted) information from what the Associated Press titled:

"Texas Governor Linked to Lethal Vaccine"

"According to an extensive investigation, Gardasil, a very controversial drug that supposedly prevents cervical cancer, was found to have caused 22 fatalities in the Austin area, along with inducing over two hundred seizures and fainting spells in that capital of Texas city. All of these incidents occurred after Texas Governor, Rick Perry filed an Executive Order to have Gardasil widely administered as a vaccine, even though its medical benefits have never been conclusively proven. But after health officials discovered the multitude of severe side-effects caused by Gardisil vaccinations, they ordered injections of it stopped, a course of action followed by Perry being thoroughly investigated for his (illegally bribed) role in the distribution of that vaccine."

As on and on the bribery goes, and where Big Pharma's buck stops, nobody seems to know. All of which is a [covering up the facts] situation that, quite conscientiously, urges me to repeat Herbert M. Shelton's, truly timeless advice:

"Let not authority be your truth, but let truth be your authority"

Yes indeed, there's nothing like the authenticity of genuine truth, especially when that level of awareness can help us overcome injury or death.

But as to the supposedly "authoritative," strictly "scientific" way of thinking, that mode of perception was famously challenged in March of 2010 when, in a Sydney, Australia hospital, the faulty judgment of two doctors was overcome by what worldwide news called:

"The Australian Kangaroo Care Miracle"

The following is a report televised by America's NBC network, an occurrence that the TV moderator called "truly miraculous." And I will now quote from an internet distributed, detailed account of that rather extraordinary event.

"Shortly after Kate Ogg gave birth to twins, although the baby girl was born quite healthy, the boy, after two doctors tried several times to get his heart to beat, he could not be revived.

And then, so Kate could reconcile herself to her deceased son (who she planned to call Jamie), a nurse placed him on his mother's chest.

But after a few minutes of tightly holding the infant, while his mother prayed for him, tearfully hoping that somehow, some way, he was still alive, a very strange thing happened: suddenly Kate's baby began to display short, somewhat spastic movements.

However, according to the pair of doctors there, the infant was simply going through what they called "post-death, muscle-reflex-actions," and to verify that prognosis, they examined him a second time, when they again found that his heart was not functioning. And so after voicing their regrets to the boy's parents, those physicians left the room, moving on to attend to other duties.

But later, when Kate was being interviewed about her son's amazing recovery, she told the TV host that, while she was holding her apparently lifeless baby, what came to mind was a magazine article about what Australian Aborigines call

"Kangaroo Care." And then she explained that, according to that report, when a kangaroo is born, while the mother holds the infant close to her chest, after a while, her heartbeat awakens her baby from the deep, deathlike sleep that Aborigines call "Spirit-Body Rebirth."

"And so that's what I did with Jamie," Kate told the TV audience. "While I held him tightly to my chest, I kept praying that my heartbeat would awaken his, and thereby give him life. And lo and behold, that's what happened."

And evidently she was telling the truth, because according to the attending nurse and her husband (both of whom were on that TV show with Kate), the longer Jamie laid across her chest, the more animated and alive he became.

"And then, I was so totally thrilled that Jamie was revived," Kate said. "I asked a nurse if she could summon the two doctors who delivered him, so that they could see that, although his heart had temporarily stopped working, he had truly overcome that malfunction."

And when one of those physicians retuned, after seeing baby Jamie's continuous movements, and then listening to his heartbeat with a stethoscope, he said:

"I just can't believe it. Your son's recovery is a miracle like . . . none that I've *ever* seen.

Then, following that, the infant was given a series of tests, mainly to determine if, while his heartbeat was too faint to detect, his lack of blood pressure may have caused mental or physical disabilities. But to his parent's gleeful delight, Jamie was found to be a fully functioning, perfectly healthy child.

Yes indeed, wonders never cease. And in my way of thinking, that true-to-life event momentously reveals the so-called "miraculous" results that can be evoked by metaphysical approaches to healing.

Therefore, despite the medical industry's massive avoidance of the spiritually evoked, prayer-linked dimension of curative powers, I continue to emphasize my belief in the following declaration:

Learning how to tap into our soul-power-connected, disease-curing abilities should, quite persistently, be a basic human right.

And speaking of vitally initiated rights, a very important rule of law to know about is the one called:

The Patient Self-Determination Act (the PSDA)

Reinstated by President Obama in 2010, what this highly significant directive does is, quite justifiably require **ALL** U.S. healthcare facilities to inform their patients about their right to refuse an unwanted treatment.

And according to the following report, a medical procedure that duly **should** be refused is the one clearly exposed in a May of 2012 issue of The Los Angeles Times, wherein this long [ignored by "mainstream news"] fact is ((quite openly)) revealed in this (quoted) article simply titled:

"The Truth About Chemotherapy

After five years of extensive research, the internationally respected Hutchinson Cancer Research Center (located in Seattle, Washington) has come to the following, well proven conclusion:

Chemotherapy treatments do *not* effectively rid a patient of cancerous cells, but instead they induce the strongest of these cells to grow and rapidly reproduce, a result that induces a reinforced form of cancer that, within 6 to 18 months, actually *causes* the patient to die."

And following that long-overdue, justified admittance, the same report reveals several diet related ways that can, quite effectively, prevent cancer from happening—an increasingly vital subject that is detailed in chapter 7 of this book.

However, despite the multitude of studies that expose the ongoing ineffectiveness of chemotherapy treatments, due to the fact that this "traditional" process has been practiced for decades, doctor's keep habitually utilizing it. All of which is the main reason why, year after year, the fatality rate of various cancers keeps rising higher—a dilemma that continually urges the need for a more progressive, less "customary" approach to defeating the second leading cause of death.

But of course, (the cutely nicknamed) "chemo" process is just one of a myriad of ways that Big Pharma's profit-based, worldwide advertising negates our self-empowering choices.

For example, the severe side-effects of (globally promoted) vaccines has become so epidemic, that in June of 2012, the U.S. government duly reinstated what has come to be called:

The Vaccine Injury Compensation Program (VICP)

This crucially needed directive was created to provide a federal system for compensating vaccination-related injuries and deaths. It is funded by a 5 percent excise tax on all vaccines sold in the United States. And since its inception, this fund (due to court-ordered compensations), has paid out over **1.7 billion dollars** to anyone made seriously ill by vaccinations. All while thousands of cases are still pending before the courts, yet to be resolved.

Therefore, before you allow yourself (or your children) to be injected with vaccines that you have no detailed information about, it makes good sense to look up that drug on the internet, whereby you can discover if it is truly safe and verified as effective.

And speaking of the (protection energy) facts available from the internet, via that quite often helpful source of information, I recently came across a healthcare law that deserves to be widely realized—a directive that the U.S. government calls:

The Emergency Medical Treatment Act (EMTA)

This significant piece of legislation is one that requires **ALL** U.S. hospitals to treat patients with emergency conditions, regardless of their ability to pay for medical services.

Although regrettably, this "anti-dumping" law is quite often violated, whereby hospitals frequently transfer emergency cases to clinics that openly serve the uninsured. However, these illegal transfers have instigated many lawsuits, and justly so, because enforcement of this mandate is a truly essential human right, regardless of race or "age" or income level.

Yes indeed, with enough public pressure, justice **will** occur not only in courtrooms, but also amid the medical arena, where treatments need to be less about profits, and more about a deeply fundamental respect for people's lives.

And with that said and ((hopefully)) practiced, I will now end this chapter by sharing a few verses from one of my (recently released) CDs—a somewhat protest-oriented song that says basically this:

In their constant push of profits, pills and stitches,
They ride a runaway train of uncontrolled riches,
All while minds fill with fear about uninsured ills,
Where heart attacks occur by just **looking** at bills,
Where a preset retirement **forces** us to quit,
But I keep on working till I'm **REALLY** done with it.
And I refuse to receive any chemical injections,
Or be fooled by the whim of uncaring inspections,
Thus I continue to avoid the surgeon's blade,
Because my body is **one** that is **truly** self-made,
Therefore I live (**within**) it, and can **see** (**inside**) it,

Whereby no harmful forces can **ever** override it,
And my human rights should **never** be denied,
By people who think they can **push** them aside,
So I keep on learning what I really **NEED to know**,
To   arouse   the   ((awareness))   that   helps   me   to
(((**GROW**)))) . . .

(((CHAPTER SEVEN)))

THE LIFE AND EARTH-((PRESERVING)), NEW ERA DIET

> "How ironical it is that we are fed by a food industry that,
> quite obviously, cares very little about our health, and
> then doctored by a healthcare industry that, for the same,
> so-called "practical" reasons, cares very little about what
> food we eat."
> —Alan Watts

Yes indeed, that's very true. And those words come from the brilliant author who, along with his Buddhism-oriented teachings, the eminent Alan Watts taught me some important facts about Hippocrates, the Greek physician who, quite famously, said this in what has come to be called The Hippocratic Oath:

> "Thy food shall be thy remedy."

Thus by transcribing timelessly beneficial truisms, although the teachings of Hippocrates were written many centuries ago, most of its basic, highly conscious principles are still being taught in medical schools throughout this planet.

However, now that the healthcare industry has become such a hugely profit making business, many of the precepts of the Hippocratic Oath have come to be disregarded, especially the parts of it that (in this widely-circulated, modernized version) say this:

> "As a doctor, I should never lose sight of the fact that warmth, sympathy, and understanding is much more important than the surgeon's knife or the chemist's drug. And above all, I must educate people about the wholesomely natural, disease preventing food that God the Creator has provided us with, because prevention is the most effective remedy."

Very good advice indeed, but I can't help to wonder if Hippocrates would cringe at how his very sensible, healthy food based ways of curing has been, quite massively, turned into a modern day motto that goes something like this:

"This delicious, double-paddy, Whopper-Burger is surely the best thing for my body."

Thus it's no wonder that, according to extensive research, as of 2012, mainly due to cholesterol-loaded, heart-attack and cancer causing diets, life expectancy (in the United States) has plunged to 48th place on this planet, its lowest rank in over fifty years.

But in order to avoid harshly criticizing what a multitude of people like to eat, I often try to share ((probably life-saving)), dietary facts by doing it sarcastically, such as what is relayed by the (sharp-witted) cartoon that I will now describe:

Several hefty-looking cattle are standing in a line, waiting to enter a place where, above its doorway, a sign says Sam's Slaughterhouse. And from the opened mouth of one of the steers, there is a caption that says:

"Anyway, after we get brutally turned into burgers and steaks, at least we get our revenge in the end, by giving people artery-clogged heart-attacks."

Oh yes, bred-for-meat cattle not only retaliate by causing a myriad of circulation problems, but also, due to the forest destruction that makes pastures to grow their food, more woodlands are leveled to feed cattle than any other tree-cutting purpose.

And yet cattle production consumes not only outrageous amounts of ecology-balancing forests, but also massive amounts of water, because it takes a **hundred times** more water to produce a pound of beef than it takes to produce a single pound of wheat. In fact, according to a very outstanding book called **Diet for a New America**, over **half** the total amount of fresh water in the U.S. goes to irrigate the land used to grow pig and cattle-feed, a startling fact echoed by this quote from **Newsweek** magazine:

> "The water that goes into producing a 600-pound, hormone-fed, beefed-up steer would float a destroyer." Now **THAT'S** a lot of precious water, far too much to be squandered, especially when water shortages have become a major dilemma throughout this planet.

Also, another environmentally damaging aspect of beef production, is the fact that it steadily pollutes streams and rivers with manure. And I mean **mucho** manure, as according to **Diet For a New America**, cattle in the U.S. produces "**twenty times** more excrement than what is produced by its entire human population."

And with that rather stunning statistic in mind, perhaps it's about time for humanity to focus on the common sense ecology emphasized by this ancient Buddhist proverb:

> "The frog does not spoil the pond in which he lives."

However, far be it for mega-rich, beef-selling companies (such as McDonalds Incorporated) to think about saving our precious waterways, or reducing the amount of fatalities caused by their overly fattening, "super-sized" burgers.

But almost as unhealthy as the constantly advertised, so-called "Big Mac Happy Meal," are the effects of the caffeine-laced, sugar-loaded colas usually consumed with them, especially if we consider the following, very significant fact:

A 12-ounce can of cola has the same effect on a 40-pound child as three cups of coffee have on a 120-pound adult.

Oh, so **that's** why little Johnny steadily wants what its contents have [addicted] him to, a continual supply of heavily caffeinated Coca-Cola. And that may also explain his nervously, inattentive behavior during his school classes, especially amid his lunch break when, the cafeteria Coke machine conveniently feeds his caffeine-habit—a craving quickly eased by two cans of [[stomach-churning]] cola.

But of course we can't blame children for yearnings massively promoted by "soft drink" campaigns, whereby soda machines (such as the one I recently saw at a mall) typically trumpet foot-high, catchy messages that beckon us to **"FEED THE RUSH!"**

And as to the relentlessly promoted, internationally waged profit-war between Pepsi and Coca-Cola, if taken to a totally ridiculous extreme, the following cartoon could actually happen:

Sitting in an office that has a large Coca-Cola logo on its wall, there is a man with a sign on his desk that says District Manager. And sitting in front of him is a fellow who looks rather sad, probably because his boss just told him this:

"Sorry Charlie, even though you're a good accountant, I'm gonna have to fire you, because unfortunately, your weekly blood-test says that you've been drinking Pepsi."

But surely the ceaselessly waged, ever-bubbling battle between Coke and Pepsi is much more serious than a cartoon-level joke, because the harmful effects of these beverages keeps entering into our lives, again and again.

For example, while on an airplane, I was vividly reminded of the (stomach-aching) indigestion caused by phosphoric acid-loaded, soda-pops, because after the boy sitting next to me quickly drank two cans of Pepsi, he vomited all over his lap and mine. And no, he didn't upchuck those colas because of "fear of flying" (as the stewardess suggested), but surely it was an outcome of the chemical-laced concoction gurgling in his stomach.

However, even if consuming "soft drinks" is pleasurable to you, keep in mind the diuretic (dehydrating) effects that these so-called "refreshments" induce. Because instead of quenching one's thirst, studies reveal that the phosphoric acid (contained in most of these beverages) creates the **diuretic** effect of making people **more** thirsty, and thereby increase sales of the product.

And as to how this thirst-making influence happens, independent laboratories have found that phosphoric acid strongly inhibits the **ADH** (anti-diuretic hormone), the vitally important, pineal secretion that activates human skin to rehydrate.

Also, in September of 2012, I read another report about the skin-damaging effects commonly induced by soda-pops. According to that globally circulated news item, research scientists in England have discovered that sodium benzoate (a preservative now added to many popular colas), seriously impairs skin cell reproduction. And I will now quote from the internet distributed article about that very controversial chemical—a report originally featured in the prestigious London Times:

"Due to a one-year study done at England's Sheffield University, it's been found that sodium benzoate, a chemical now contained in Coca-Cola, Pepsi, Sprite and Fanta, is an ingredient that seriously mutates the DNA of epidermal tissue, and thereby can cause skin cancer."

And along with that dangerous side-effect, the massive amount of sugar in these beverages is a major cause of diabetes, plus of course, as most of us realize, sugar-loaded drinks commonly induce tooth decay, thereby creating the Sugar Blues Bill from the man with the drill.

All of which brings us to the realization of this vitally significant fact:

Surely the time has come for these [burgers-and-colas], so-called "Happy Meals" to be seen for what they **really** are: a well propagandized, illness-causing food that, quite sensibly, should be minimized.

And speaking of overcoming widely problematic advertising, there's an ongoing, meat-industry-pushed proclamation that gets continually spread, a common misconception that says basically this:

"Vegetarians are weaker and have less energy than meat eaters"

But to accurately dispute that erroneous belief, I will point out some basic, Nature-proven facts of life:

First of all, if vegetarians are **truly** weaker (and less energetic) than meat eaters, then why are some of the strongest, quickest and most lively animals sustained by plant-based diets, mammals such as horses, zebras and antelope?

Also, in regard to the longevity factor, the longest living mammal is the hugely strong elephant, a strictly vegetarian being that lives **seven to eight times longer** than carnivores such as house cats, dogs, lions and tigers.

And along with that true-to-life reality, be aware that fruits and vegetables digest in about an hour, while meat takes over four hours, which is mainly why (strictly meat-eating) animals do so much sleeping, because the intensity of the digestion process consumes a lot of their energy.

And as to the human realm, of the 18 most decorated Olympic stars, 12 of them won their medals while being vegetarians—a list of people that includes world renown tennis stars, Serena and Venus Williams, along with the legendary Olympian sprinters, Carl Lewis and Edwin Moses.

However, even though I'm well aware of the energy-producing benefits of avoiding meat in my diet, I do occasionally eat fish, mostly to provide the basic need for vitamins B-6 and B-12. But because I live very near the sea (a five-minute walk from a village where fisherman catch fresh fish daily), I only eat what comes directly from the ocean, and thereby avoid most of the bacteria content of seafood sold at markets.

Also, largely due to its vitamin A, D, B-1 and B-2 content, plus its copious amount of calcium, I often eat one scrambled egg for breakfast (one that's usually covered with vitamin-packed, green olives, and then sandwiched between slices of protein-rich, whole wheat bread).

But as to keeping a bone-strengthening supply of calcium in your body, be very careful about taking pills that supposedly fulfill that need, because recent studies about those capsules reveal that, quite often, an overload of calcium can clog-up bloodstream flow, and thereby cause heart attacks.

And to duly verify the health endangering effects of taking calcium pills, I will now quote from a widely distributed report about that dilemma, an important news item released by the **British Medical Journal** titled:

"A DIETARY AND MEDICAL ALERT:
Beware of the Often Lethal Effects of Calcium Supplements"

"A five-year study conducted by The British Medical Journal involved 1,472 women, all of whom were from 65 to 75 years old. Half of the participants took one (500 mg) calcium-filled capsule a day, while the other half took merely a placebo.

And the results of this research discovered the following, momentous fact:

The women assigned to take calcium supplements experienced **twice** the amount of heart attacks than those who took a placebo."

And then that report went on to say this:

"Because of the artery-clogging dangers involved with ingesting overloads of calcium supplements, we of The British

Medical Journal highly recommend that those pills be avoided, as it is much safer to get your bone-strengthening needs from the following (high in calcium-content) foods:

Potatoes, green peppers, cabbage, broccoli, papayas, bananas and coconuts, just to name a few."

Thus by reading that article, I recently decided to forgo eating eggs, and instead get calcium from what's growing in my yard, because all of the foods mentioned in that report are, quite thankfully, available from the Zion House garden.

Yes, being the diehard "survivalist" that I am, for the past five years I've been fervently cultivating fruit trees and vegetables, all of which produce what my family and I like to eat. And also, dozens of large coconut trees were, to my delight, scattered amid this lovely, five-acre patch of land when I bought it, along with a myriad of ((Creator given)) papaya and banana trees.

Note: the sweet liquid that comes from the center of a coconut is, according to various studies, one of the most vitamin-enriched substances on this planet, and drinking it also has a potently rejuvenating effect on skin. And even though coconuts mainly grow in tropical areas, they are often sold in the markets of northern climate cities.

Also, coconuts produce what has been found to be the most healthily, cholesterol-free type of cooking oil.

Yet another of Nature's ((gifts)) to well being is the papaya, the very nutritious fruit produced by a truly amazing plant that, with a good amount of rain (or manual watering), has the astonishing ability to grow from seed to ripened fruit in little more than a year.

Also, another quickly grown (and vitally nutritious) fruit are bananas, the offspring of a plant so stunningly tenacious that, even if it gets blown down by a storm, it quickly sprouts a new tree, soon to reproduce what has come to be called "Nature's Perfect Food." And surely it deserves that recognition, because bananas provide the following, highly beneficial vitamins, minerals and calcium:

Vitamins A, B-1, B-2, B-3, B-6, B-9 and C, plus **lots** of energy-bringing potassium, niacin and carbohydrates.

Thus with the Creator's ongoing, body-saving salvations steadily in mind, I will now conclude this chapter by offering this food-based, (hopefully) educational verse from a song that I call:

Living the ((Naturally)) Homegrown Life

To avoid the pesticides of corporate-grown **food,**
eat what is **organic** and **wholesomely good,**
Because food is a friend that we **can't** leave for **long,**
so it should be a companion that **won't** do us **wrong,**
And if you have a yard, perhaps the time has **arrived,**
to make a garden that helps you and yours **survive,**
a place where Nature's food is ((**ceaselessly growing**)),
blessed by the cultivation that keeps it all ((**flowing**)),
A labor of love that feeds both **body and soul,**
as being **Earth-FRIENDLY** is a ((**life-SAVING**)) **goal** . . .

(((CHAPTER EIGHT)))

((PROTECTION ENERGY)) VERSUS EXCESS STRESS

"You have a brain in your head, and feet in your shoes, and
you can steer yourself in any direction you choose."
—Dr. Seuss

Yes indeed, by believing in the basic truth of that charming
piece of verse, I've steered myself into the stress-reducing,
metaphysical dimension that I call ((Spirit-Linked-Protection-
Energy)).

But of course, alleviating blood-pressure-raising, overloads
of tension is something that most of us deal with every day,
especially if we live a busily, hard-working life. Therefore,
to maintain one's healthy well being, it's important to learn
effective ways to do what I call:

Tuning-Up the Tension Tamer

Surely we **all** encounter situations that make us angrily
impatient, intensely stressful moments that, for the most part,
happen when we're in a nervous hurry. Perhaps an eruption of
severe [[inner-pressure]] might occur when you're late for an
important appointment, or when stuck in rush-hour traffic—a
predicament that might make you feel like your blood is boiling.

Oh gosh, I'm talking about panicky times when your entire body feels like its screaming **WHAT'S THE !ô#?! HOLD UP?!**

But to avoid (potentially heart attack causing), fury-filled situations, doing something as simple as (humming a tune) can be a helpful compression-reliever, whereby a little bit of (internal musicality)) can overcome an untimely bout with erupting ferocity.

Or as the legendary calamity-calmer, Bob Marley was known to say:

> "Let sweet music help your troubles fade away, because
> if you didn't love yourself, would you **still** be here today?"

As (spirit-guided) Marley again reminds us that, no matter what problem is troubling you, there's always the open door into one's (peaceful inner-core), whereby you don't "save" your soul—**IT** saves **YOU** from [dangerous overloads of stress].

"Salvation is revealed to contemplative, thoughtful beings," wrote the eminent metaphysician, Honore de Balzac, an author who penned a multitude of timeless insights that, via the power of perceptive thinking, has helped millions of people sooth their worries.

But unfortunately, nowadays, most doctors are "too busy" to teach ways to avoid the [flying-off-the handle], chronic rage that causes heart failure and strokes, mainly because that level of education involves the "impracticality" of instructing methods of ((**perpetual prevention**)).

All of which is a dilemma that makes me wonder if medical facilities can somehow be updated, whereby they can justifiably deal with what I call **The Lack of Peace of Mind Disease**, a [life-threatening] attitude now becoming increasingly epidemic.

And yet, apparently, there **is** some soothingly tension-relieving changes happening amid the healthcare industry, as I recently read a news item stating that, in September of 2012, a California-based medical school began offering courses in what I've been doing for decades: the process that I call C.E. Massage and Talk Therapy. But according to that internet-circulated report, the professor teaching that class calls it "Massage Merged With Self-Healing Psychology." However, regardless of what that technique is named, what **really** matters is its truly beneficial results.

Also, in regard to the therapeutic effects of massage-connected, (inner-spirit-linked) levels of healing, I recently saw a TV news broadcast about a newly established expansion of that process. According to that televised report, the city governments (of Chicago and Los Angeles) have decided to employ members of a company called:

M.E.L.T. (Massage Emergency Life-Preserver Teams)

What initially launched the M.E.L.T. organization, was the fact that, mainly due to the inner-city, [unreleased pressure] of their job, police officers frequently develop what is called a "hot-wired temper." And what that "trigger-happy" condition does is, all too often, cause them to shoot (quite often lethally) any suspect who, for whatever reason, is fleeing from the scene of a crime, a perhaps (stress-induced), over-reaction that has come to be called "instant execution."

Therefore, to lessen the amount of lawsuits and (innocent bystander) complaints that arise from that dilemma, due to the fact that massage effectively quells [stored-up], violent reactions to a situation, several inner-city police departments hired the services of the M.E.L.T. organization. All of which involves a process that, quite firmly **requires** urban streets patrolling, law enforcement officers to get twice-a-week, free-of-charge, full-body massages.

And after receiving six months of ((stress-subduing)) rub-downs, a technique administered to over two hundred Los Angeles and Chicago policemen, studies found that those massages caused a **90 percent** drop in those city's (police-initiated) gunfire. And hopefully, due to their truly beneficial results, Massage Emergency Life-Preserver Teams will get increasingly utilized in metropolitan areas worldwide.

But of course tension-induced, infuriated reactions not only occur in big cities, but all throughout society, where explosive behavior is steadily spurred by [[media-pushed]] barrages of gun-play scenes, a frame of mind getting more and more widespread, especially in the U.S.

For example, during April of 2012, in the small town of Chardon, Ohio, a 17 year-old boy, while standing inside a high school cafeteria, for a totally unexplained reason, shot and killed three students, along with seriously wounding two others. But due to the fact that these victims were completely unknown to the boy who attacked them, what **really** caused his homicidal outburst? Was it mostly triggered by nightmare-causing, bloody films that massive amounts of people get exposed to **every day**?

And then, a few months after that Ohio tragedy, truly obvious proof of the effects of violent movies occurred when, yet another American student went on a so-called "unprovoked" killing spree, a tragically widespread one that happened in the town of Aurora, Colorado. That woeful incident, as you may recall, happened when a post-graduate, male college student broke into the back door of a movie theater (where hundreds of people sat watching a very violent "Batman" film). And then, this well educated, 24 year-old, white American, while firing a (100-bullet-firing), assault rifle, shot 71 strangers, killing 12 and wounding 59.

As on and on it goes, yet another "mysteriously unexplainable," senseless massacre. But according to news broadcasts about the Aurora, Colorado catastrophe, the shooter, James Holmes, imagined himself as being "The Joker," a homicidal maniac often featured in "Batman" movies. Thus Holmes became a clearly blatant example of the [[rage-erupting]], murderous effects of violent films and videos.

All of which points to an increasingly dire situation that, quite urgently, needs to be alleviated by a multifaceted approach to violence-quelling education, a way of conscientious teaching that, at long last, can counteract the explosive programming that keeps people steadily—

Under the Gunpace

Years ago, due to my connections with the Whole Life Expo organization, I was hired to host a Los Angeles-based, TV special, during which I interviewed a panel of doctors who, along with their standard medical practices, they specialized in stress-relieving techniques.

At that time I was living in Hawaii, and after flying to Los Angeles to appear on that nationally televised program, while taking a taxi to a hotel, I saw, for the the first time, the bright red letters of that eerie word, **Gunpace** (spray-painted on the wall of a building).

Then, after entering the third floor suite reserved for me, feeling somewhat jangled from that 65 miles-per-hour, [[weaving-through-freeway traffic]] ride in that taxicab, I couldn't get that **Gunpace** word out of my mind.

However, realizing that I had only a few hours to (pull myself together) for a TV show, being the genuine Youthman Messenger that I am, I needed to quickly release any [agitation-caused] "aging" from my face. And so I firmly massaged it with some bottled water, all while (whispering to myself) an **Inner Directions** invocation that, (as you may recall from Chapter 2), says basically this:

"Be here **now**, Jesse, be here tension-free, worry-free, pain-free and wrinkles-free. And remember, **YOU** are **TOTALLY** in control of your body."

And then, after that procedure, when I opened the curtain to see the view, I saw something that was quite memorable: skillfully covering a wall (across the street), was a huge mural, a painting that depicted the faces of three of my favorite people: Pablo Picasso, Thomas Edison and Benjamin Franklin.

At first glance, it was the radiantly expressive face of Picasso that caught my eye, having long been an admirer of that man who, even at 90 years "old," was physically strong and creatively productive—he the anti-war activist who brought new consciousness to the world of modern art.

And to the right of Pablo's face was Thomas Edison, the ingenious innovator who saw the shining light within himself, followed by him brilliantly inventing an electrified version of it. But Edison also pioneered the phonograph, plus the motion picture camera, along with being a popular public speaker, whereby he would gather large crowds to hear his philosophic advice. He the man with shining eyes who I quoted in my *Awareness* magazine column as saying:

> "The most effective doctors prescribe no medicine, but instead they educate people about the actual causes of disease and depression."

Thus Edison was much more than an extraordinary inventor, because he also gifted humanity with helpful insights about the human body, a man who, even at 84 years of age, was still actively exploring breakthrough discoveries. And there he was again, resonating back into my consciousness, Edison the Enlightener, beaming a peaceful smile that subdued the hustle and bustle of that traffic-packed street.

And then I focused on the face of the revolutionary author, physics researcher, civic activist, musician, composer, satirist, international speaker and diplomat, the uniquely comprehensive, Renaissance Man, Benjamin Franklin. And although his famous face graces the American hundred dollar bill, Franklin's true worth is priceless, because not only was he a brilliant philosopher and world famous ambassador, but he also pioneered some of the original experiments with what we now call "electricity."

And with that trio of international innovators still in my mind, I was inspired to mention them during that TV show, when I urged the panel of doctors there to discuss the vital needs of progressive forms of consciousness, especially when it involves the art of stress-reducing, metaphysical healing.

Then, while we answered questions from the audience there, to spice things up (as I often like to do), I tossed-in a few (hopefully) tension-taming ticklers, such as the Richard Lewis gag about his grandfather, "the Jewish juggler who worried about six things at once."

And along with utilizing a dash of sarcasm to ease the crowd's nervousness, I also quelled my own timidity by walking among the audience (while shaking many of their hands), all while realizing that a friendly handshake is, of course, a very effective tension reliever.

But along with the (malice-mellowing) effects of kindly modes of touch, there is a flip-side to that process that makes stress-release a double-edged sword. On the one hand, we don't want to raise blood-pressure with a rage that causes illness, but on the other hand, it's physically and mentally damaging to let infuriation fester inside, ceaselessly unrelieved.

And so we need to occasionally counterbalance our need to stay calm and collected by letting off some steam, because cardiologists identify two types of stress, a significant duality that is explained as follows:

The first (and most dangerous) mode of stress is called the "hot-reactor" type, that which occurs when the brain and blood-pressure over-react to stimuli. But less obvious is the "highly-resistant" type of stressful tension, a [fury-fostering] frame of mind that occurs when intensely felt anger is too long suppressed.

However, according to research done at the Harvard School of Public Health, the following method was discovered to be a very effective hostility-reliever, a process that is described by the following, internet released report:

"After conducting a two-year study of the ill effects of long-withheld resentment and depression, we discovered that, by occasionally relieving their outrage by publicly protesting against wrongdoings, that group of people had much lower blood-pressures, along with far fewer illnesses."

Or as the world renown peace-activist, Walt Whitman said in a proclamation he titled:

"The Ultimate Solution"

"If by some sort of miraculous, act-of-God decree, murder is truly outlawed throughout this planet, then only outlaws will be able to start wars. And by realizing that, massive peace demonstrations will thereby become a truly righteous, openly public way to emphasize our legal protection against lawbreakers. And if elected officials cannot tolerate protests against the brutality of warfare, then they too, like any other mass murderer, should stand trial for their heinous crimes."

However, for those of you not inclined to release [stored-up] outrage via public protest, or by writing educational, peace-promoting letters to the media, there are many simply (physical) ways to ease overloads of [inner-turbulence], a technique that I simply call:

The Whack-Attack

Although it's more commonly done by men, either gender can relieve excessive amounts of stress by harmlessly hitting a ball—be it a tennis ball, golf ball, baseball, racquet ball or billiard balls, whatever it takes to release heart-straining levels of blood-pressure.

But to get these tension-taming methods to really work for you, they need to be done on a **regular** basis (which is why I bought a pool table, whereby I release suppressed irritation by whacking porcelain balls around, usually for about a half-hour a day).

Also, along with harmlessly hitting things, I've discovered the hostility-healing results of playing a musical instrument, an effective stress-buster that I activate by ((pounding-out)) notes on an electric piano, sometimes alone, and sometimes with my reggae band. All while realizing that playing a musical instrument causes blissfully uplifting, therapeutic ((brain-waves)) that, according to electronic, mind-scanning studies, only (self-made) music can produce.

But as to the basic need to quell unreleased anxiety and agitation, I see it as a healthcare process that should be increasingly developed, whereby humanity can, quite appropriately, learn to subdue a major cause of heart attacks and physical decay.

And with that proclamation said and ((hopefully utilized)), I will now wrap up this chapter with a verse from one of my songs—a message that focuses on what is probably the most effective rage-reliever of all—the eminently peace-bringing process simply called:

FORGIVENESS

If you learn to let grudges be duly **released**—
Your mind and body will be **blessed with PEACE**—
Enabling you to spark-up your self-healing ((**might**))—
Soothing away anger with your ((**curative light**))—
Arousing your wellness via ((**POSITIVITY**))—
Keeping you aimed at your **BEST** ((**DESTINY**))) . . .

(((CHAPTER NINE)))

THE NEW ERA OF LONGEVITY HAS ARRIVED

Oh yes, it certainly has, all throughout this planet, and that significant advancement can healthfully endure, especially when people realize that ((love of life)) should be a ceaseless process, one that begins when we are born into this amazingly interesting world.

And I see evidence of newly found, (glad-to-be-alive)) energy every day, especially while watching the delightful exuberance that my 2-year "old" son reveals, a radiant joy that arises even after he stumbles and falls, because a few seconds later, he's up again, beaming that (Original Grin).

Thus he helpfully reminds me that the (stumbling-and-getting-back-up), learning process is the ((central activator)) of human longevity, moving us forward from one challenging experience to another, with every year a newly achieved, worthy accomplishment.

And speaking of progressive accomplishments, after reading "The Longevity Revolution"—a brilliantly informative book written by the Pulitzer Prize winning author, Dr. Robert N. Butler—I have decided to dedicate a large portion of this chapter to him.

Quite clearly, what Dr. Butler has done for the well being of humanity is worth reading about, not only due to his truly beneficial books, but also because of his achievements as the

steadily dedicated, hard-working founder of the International
Longevity Center (the duly praised I.L.C.).

For example, during his ten years as President of that
organization, one of his most effective duties was to give
twice-weekly classes to an auditorium filled with doctors
and medical students—sessions that teach the facts that
medical practitioners really **need** to know. And the following
classroom lecture, (one that was taped and then distributed
via the internet), is a memorable sample of Dr. Butler's truly
educational knowledge:

> "Studies show that how long we live has very
> little to do with the use of medicines or surgery, but it
> mostly comes from efforts to create a more positive,
> self-empowered image of the aging process. Also, along
> with the help of self-esteem-lifting psychology, lifespan
> throughout this planet has been greatly lengthened
> by improvements in basic housing needs for the poor
> and elderly. But with all things considered, along
> with the life-extending effects of quelling overloads
> of stress-induced tension, a central factor of increased
> longevity is, quite crucially, increasing awareness of the
> **true** effects of what we commonly eat and drink. Thus
> largely due to what has become the widely accepted,
> American diet, I will again remind you that, during the
> last thirty years, life expectancy in the U.S. has been
> rapidly descending, so much so, that it's now dropped to
> a shameful 48th place on this planet. However, as long
> as I am director of the International Longevity Center, I
> promise to do **all** that I can to bring this country's health
> and life expectancy back up to international standards.
> And one way that this institute will do that is, first of
> all, by funding nationally televised documentaries aimed
> at increasing this country's shamefully neglected lack of
> healthcare education. And along with that, to decrease
> the outrageously high prices of medical procedures in

the U.S., I promise to steadily forward the ability of this Longevity Center to offer **truly** affordable, healthcare services. Yes, that's our **real** duty as genuinely humane, medical practitioners, especially when it comes to taking proper care of our precious senior citizens, especially those who are greedily victimized by doctor's fees that, far too often, are thousands of dollars more than what an uninsured patient is able to pay."

And surely Dr. Butler did a lot to make his intensions a reality, whereby he initiated so many vitally needed services for the elderly that, to do him justice, I've provided the following list that, (quite briefly) describes some of what his leadership of the International Longevity Center (I.L.C.) achieved:

1. The I.L.C. has implemented worldwide, free-of-charge classes that teach working ways to overcome the myriad of prejudices that, for many decades, have kept a depressingly ageism-oriented, unhealthy grip on the mentality of so-called "uselessly retired" people.

2. In 2009, the I.L.C. strongly urged President Obama to alleviate the disgraceful dilemma that, largely due to the health-budget cuts of George W. Bush, over 28 million U.S. senior citizens lost their medical insurance. But fortunately, due to President Obama's ceaseless efforts to make medical services available to the uninsured elderly, as of December, 2012, that basic human right was officially made into law.

3. The I.L.C. has thoroughly reformed dozens of shoddily run "old folks" homes in the U.S., doing so after studies found that majority of these facilities, quite covertly, had less than **half** the number of on-call staff that federal guidelines deem as being minimally necessary.

4. The I.L.C. has become an agency duly aimed at alleviating the following, quite disturbing fact: more than 40 percent of suicides are committed by persons

65 or older—a dilemma largely caused by increases in so-called "senile dementia." And yet, according to Dr. Butler's research teams, quite frequently, "senile dementia" is a condition caused by the side-effects of so-called "anti-depressant" pills. But to justifiably counteract that situation, I.L.C. attorneys filed criminal charges against pharmaceutical companies that, quite repeatedly, refused to stop selling drugs that frequently induce suicidal behavior.

5. Between 2001 and 2008, to overcome the fact that the Bush administration spent less than 1 cent of every tax dollar on disease prevention, the I.L.C. gave nationwide, cost-free, 2-day seminars that teach truly working ways to avoid illness, frailty, and life-threatening bouts of depression.

And that is just a small sample of the steadily ongoing, Longevity Center services that (hopefully) help people live longer, healthier and happier lives.

However, along with what government-supported agencies can do, there still remains the need to personally, spiritually and psychologically come to grips with this increasingly important question:

Why Should the "Normal" Lifespan of Human Beings Be Extended?

To provide some comprehensive answers to this vital probe into the significance of life, I offer this list of three reasons to ((joyfully)) live as long as possible:

Reason Number (1):

More than anything else, people need to transcend the ageist fallacy that "old folks" are an "unproductive" drain on the basic needs of humanity, but the actual truth is this: over 80 percent of circulated money flows from "senior citizens" to younger people.

And with that substantial benefit in mind, as long as I can maintain a healthfully fit and ((continually learning)) existence, I would like to live for at least 120 years, or even longer, depending on the condition that I'm in. And amid a (spirit-linked) lifestyle, perhaps that is not a far-fetched desire, because according to the supposedly true-to-life, Genesis part of the Bible, back when the most trusted cure was the healing energy of "God the Creator," many people lived longer than two centuries. But of course, that was then and this is **now.** And yet, by ((connecting)) with the same spirituality that enabled those amazingly long lives, surely that ability can also ((re-energize)) **us**, whereby a New Era of Consciousness can, to a large extent, make the 21st century the very best time to live on planet Earth.

Or as the world renown metaphysician, poet and philosopher, Kahlil Gibran declared: "All that good spirits desire, good spirits attain, because the Spiritual World is the source of infinite possibilities."

Reason Number (2):

Although companies often require people to "retire" at the age of 65, of course, that doesn't mean we should stop working, because by being freed from a rigidly restricted schedule, we then have the time to delightfully focus on art-making projects. Therefore, by deeply connecting with a creative activity, along with activating the ((body-regenerating energy)) of the human mind, we also tap-into the truly captivating, (inventive dimension) that, whenever we choose to make a work of art, we are thereby able to make "time" fly by like it doesn't exist.

Or as the famously ageless artist, Grandma Moses was quoted as saying (when she was 101):

> "Live the timeless life of your creative soul, steadily rejuvenated by the beauty of life and its beneficially transformative, ongoing potentials."

Reason Number (3):

Living longer lives will give us more opportunities to travel, whereby we can learn about cultures unfamiliar to us—all of which is a truly working way to keep us from becoming too [stiffly] nationalized. Thus to overcome prejudicial notions about so-called "weird foreigners," there is only one "nation" that I truly believe in, the ceaseless ((**emanation**)) of the life-sustaining, **UNIVERSAL** energy that unifies soul and mind and body.

And so let us live on and on, and **enjoy the journey**, perpetually uplifted by realizing what this hopefully ((faith-expanding)) poem of mine emphasizes—the resonating reality that—

> A New Era of Consciousness has **now greatly ARRIVED,**
> Whereby our ((**TRUE**)) longevity will be **duly REVIVED,**
> Freeing us from the [cage] of a ["life expectancy"]—
> Amid which [numbered] presets wrongly stifle our liberty—
> But instead of living in fear, *worried* that death is near—
> We should live **JOYOUSLY** long via a (**NEW FRONTIER**))) . . . .

(((CHAPTER TEN)))

((PUTTING IT ALL TOGETHER))

"The gifts of spiritual, mental and physical powers comes
from The Creator of the Universe, so be sure to honor
them well."
—Nikola Tesla

Mainly because Mr. Tesla has provided a proclamation that, quite memorably, (puts together) what this chapter is all about, I have chosen it to be its opening statement.

And to refresh your memory of some of the hopefully ((consciousness expanding)) discoveries exposed within this multifaceted book, this section provides a brief summary of the parts of it that, due to their helpfully therapeutic effects, deserve a second look. All while we keep in mind that, amid the process of watching television ("info" quickly passes by in a flash), but printed pages enable us to re-read passages that are beneficially important.

Therefore, steadily urged by my ever-learning mind, I have discovered books penetrating enough to be completely read over and over, and even if that (indelibly memorable) paperback gets battered around its edges, that's okay, because it can still be used as a ((wisdom containing)) life-saver.

And so let us again consider the exploratory importance of what I call:

Planet Earth's Biggest Mystery

Scientific studies have found that our bodies continually regenerate at the rate of about 150 million new cells a minute, whereby we are ceaselessly repaired and renewed by our healing energy. But if that is basically true, then why are diseases so often incurable, and why does our immunity, along with various bodily organs, deteriorate with age?

As we are again faced with this Mystery of Mysteries, an enigma that, (as you may recall), brings to mind what I have pointed out as being:

The Duo of Triumphant Truths

(1). The most helpful parts of the human body are the immunity and regeneration systems, and the more we learn about the ((glisteningly healing energy)) within us, the more disease-free we will be, and the brighter we will shine.

(2). Due to the fallacy that people have very little control over our self-restoring powers, learning truly effective ways to maintain mental and physical rejuvenation should, quite clearly, be our most precious human right.

Thus with that duo of truths again brought to our attention, we are duly reminded that mental strength can, quite potently, change things for the better, because nothing on Earth can replace the vitally needed, curative effects of the steadily revivified mind.

Or as the often quoted writer of classic truisms, Jalal Rumi put it:

"Although some say that human knowledge is just a drop in the ocean, if persistently expanded to its deepest potential, it becomes the entire ocean in one drop."

And speaking of the ocean-sized subject of ((healing and protective energies)), to comprehensively explain that multi-leveled realm, I have divided it into ten chapters—ten pieces of the **Spiritual-Physical-Duality-Puzzle** that are briefly described by the following summations:

CHAPTER ONE: The central theme of that chapter is to, step-by-step, increase your ability to perpetuate the (creational-energy-initiated), self-renewing powers of ((**your precious mind**)).

CHAPTER TWO: The main intent of that section is to reveal what I call the **You-nity** and **Inner-Directions** methods, both of which are regeneration-stimulating techniques that, if persistently developed, can capably self-renew and revitalize ((**your precious body**)).

CHAPTER THREE: The basic mission of that chapter is to feature true-to-life, authentic examples of people who have accomplished amazing agelessness, whereby their enlightening methods, quite effectively, teach ways to stimulate the **true** potency of ((**your rejuvenating abilities**)).

CHAPTER FOUR: The main purpose of that chapter is to accurately describe experiences that, in various ways, reveal the phenomenon that I call (protection-energy)—a potentially life-saving dimension evoked by shifting into ((**your spirit-linked powers**)).

CHAPTER FIVE: The principal objective of that section is to explore the truly therapeutic effects of making art, and thereby ((delightfully)) activate the self-renewing influences of ((**your inborn creativity**)).

CHAPTER SIX: The central goal of that chapter is to expose erroneous medical procedures that, by being habitually overdone, their "traditionally" [Old Era] methods, all too often, disregard [and therefore diminish] the powers of ((**your vitally self-curing skills**)).

CHAPTER SEVEN: The primary purpose of that chapter is to teach Earth-friendly, health-sustaining ways to feed and energize ((**your precious flesh and bones**)).

CHAPTER EIGHT: The basic intention of that section is to make known various ways to alleviate blood-pressure-rising, overloads of stress and tension—all while emphasizing the importance of preventing an excess of strain on ((**your preciously beating heart**)).

CHAPTER NINE: The initial purpose of that chapter is to reveal the widely initiated, positive effects of the International Longevity Center, followed by helping you discover significant reasons to greatly extend ((**your joyously long life**)).

CHAPTER TEN: The central aim of this chapter is to summarize and clarify some of the most important revelations explored within this book, whereby you are again re-minded about truly effective ways to fulfill ((**your perpetually evolving destiny**)) . . .

Oh yes, if ((open-mindedly)) explored, this book does all that, and **more**.

But of course, there are always the Skeptic Tankers who insist that (spirit-linked), healing and protective powers are "unscientific" and "unproven." However, I again emphasize that **results are results,** and what works once can work **THOUSANDS** of times, especially when successful methods increase our awareness of the truly universal, crucial abilities of the human mind.

And with that said, let me share with you a quote that highlights the eminent wisdom of Mahatma Gandhi, he who was quoted as saying:

> "The way I see it, the central, most significant point of being alive is to become as universally conscious as possible."

Oh yes, now **there's** a statement that totally agrees with my sensibilities, a way of thinking that will steadily ((echo)) within me, because the more I learn about the universe both (within) and ((all around me)), the more I will be remembered for, even if I live to be 150.

But oh gosh, there I go again, [pigeon-holed] by the notion that my body should be labeled by a [debilitating] cage of [numbing-numbers]. And so I will duly re-mind myself (and **you too**) that one's "age" can be perceived in one of two ways:

We can either be a **D.O.W.N.**—a [**D**umped **O**n **W**ith **N**umbers] victim, or an **U.P.**—a creatively **U**nnumbered **P**erson. And as Unnumbered People, perhaps we can view the future of our bodies in a more positive light, whereby it's not about the amount of "years" we have lived, but **HOW** we have lived them. All while we stay aware that numbers, although they are good for making lists and payments, they are a self-degrading and [unnatural] thing to be labeled with, mainly because one's physical appearance is an ((**individual**)) creation. As more and more I realize that, as a way to ((inner-spark)) one's individuality, God The Creator, quite amazingly, makes every human being's face somewhat uniquely different, whereby it's not (**exactly**) the same as anyone else's on this planet.

But unfortunately, if we fail to develop the inborn, ((self-creating)) power of our uniqueness, we thereby fall prey to the greedily profit-based, "conventional" system of [medical ageism] that, for far too long, reaps most of its financial success via this steadily programmed belief:

The bigger the the ["age" number], the bigger the doctor bills." All of which is a part of what I call:

The Increasingly Controlling Numbers Factor

Initially, for most of the residents of North America and Europe, The Numbers Factor begins very early in life, as people are then, quite "customarily" labeled with a multi-digit, so-called "Social Security" number. And then, following that, upon attending elementary school, students usually get prematurely labeled with a number that is supposedly one's "Intelligence Quotient" (IQ). And of course, upon reaching grade 6 or 7, we start to get history ("his story?) lessons, most of which consist of memorizing what year famous military battles occurred, dates such as the 6 weeks-long, 1944 to 1945 Battle of the Bulge. And then by grade 10 or 11, comes an important (to our mobility) number—16—a digit that usually enables people to get a driver's license—followed by trying to figure out how to buy a car (probably because "daddy" refuses to lend a new driver his). Anyway, the older we get, the more the numbers pile-up, whereby we memorize such things as bank machine "PIN" (**P**ersonal **I**dentity **N**umbers), along with keeping track of various telephone numbers and credit card numbers—and even, oh gosh, the number of shopping days left until Christmas! And nowadays, like it or not, there's even the prejudicial habit of grading people from 1 to 10 (according to one's physical "looks"). And of course, how can we forget the [debilitating digit] that, with each year, gets more and more burdensome—the preconceived, vastly overrated [number] of our so-called "age."

However, as to being overly [depressed] by the [[blanket generality]] of a numerical label, let me share with you a potent quote about that, a delightful remark made by the author and actress, Joan Collins—the outspoken anti-ageism activist who was quoted as saying this:

> "Despite the notion that so-called 'elderly' people are, for the most part, ill-tempered and unfriendly, the way I see it is this: no matter what your age is, the only time that you are fully dressed is when, along with your clothes, you also wear a smile."

Yes, indeed, I totally agree with that charming piece of advice, especially since I've discovered that a smile, if emanated at the start of my day, is more ((positively energizing)) than the caffeine in a cup of coffee or tea.

Thus by blissfully realizing the effects of staying positive and active, although I'm now labeled as [68], by willfully developing the methods that I utilize and teach, I feel more alive than ever before. All of which is a result greatly helped by the **Inner-Directions** techniques that, quite persistently, remind me of the following truism:

Regardless of all the "birthdays" that we accumulate, by repeatedly practicing self-renewing abilities, not only do we stimulate the health of so-called "inevitably decaying" brain-cells, we steadily re-mind ourselves that every day really **IS** a true-to-life, ((perpetually regenerating)) **REBIRTHDAY!**

And as to scientific research about ways to activate ongoing, total renewal of every "cell" one's body, quite recently, extensive studies (done by the International Longevity Center) have proven that (inner-voiced) directions can, very effectively, maximize the healing powers of our DNA. Therefore, due to the magnitude of that progressively ((forward looking)), scientific breakthrough, I find it to be one of the most significant discoveries in human history.

All of which calls to mind the world renown research of Dr. Alexis Carrel, the **Nobel Prize** winner (mentioned earlier in this book). And in regard to his monumental importance, I will again share with you this (quoted) section of Dr. Carrel's **Nobel** acceptance speech:

> **"Amid the natural process of regeneration, if human brain cells are continually supplied with the mental energy that enables them to steadily activate cellular restoration, as far as we know, total-body renewal can last for an unlimited, yet to be discovered amount of time."**

But of course, experiments that involve the ((life-preserving)) communications of the human mind go back for several centuries. For example, consider what a book about the history of the Roman Empire calls:

King Frederick's Unique Test of Word Powered, Brain Stimulation

As we now rewind (for a few moments) back to the 13th century when, largely due to his (somewhat unlimited) power over the people in his domain, Roman emperor, King Frederick conducted what turned out to be a very tragic experiment.

Basically, it was a procedure aimed at discovering what would happen if, according to emperor Frederick's instructions, a group of five newly born babies were taken care of only by their breastfeeding mothers, all while they were kept in one small room. And along with that, all five of those women were ordered not to speak even one word to their infants, or even to the other mothers there, whereby only their babies would be permitted to vocalize sounds. All of which was a King Frederick-invented, supposedly "scientific" way to find out how that situation would affect those newborn children. Would they be limited to only crying when hungry for milk? Or as a way to communicate, would they utter sounds similar to their parent's language?

However, that bizarrely strange test proved to be far more cruel than "Almighty" Frederick imagined. Cruel indeed, because after keeping those infants in that [strictly muted] room for nearly six months, apparently due to a total lack of ((word-powered)), brain activation, four out of five of those babies died!

But of course, that was a very [inhumane] way to uncover the effects that helpfully expressed, human communication has on a newborn's sense of well being, whereby a basic, psychological need is vitally fulfilled.

Alright then, with that (beneficially communicating) realization hopefully ((internalized)), now that we have reached the end of this book, I would like to give my heartfelt **thanks to YOU**, dear reader, for sharing this (word-turned-to-deed) merger with me. And I sincerely hope that this ((linking-up)) of body, intellect and spirit has brought about a lifelong, mind-to-mind friendship between us—an undying connection that, in my musical style, I will now sum up with this song I call:

VIA THIS BOOK

We have explored self-renewing powers from **A to Z**—
Whereby we keep **regenerating** ((**voluntarily**))—
Steadily mended by ((**inner-sparked-energy**))—
That heals and firms-up skin by evoking **You-nity**—
While it also cures ills with ((**word-powered-directions**))—
And defends you with ((**spirit-linked protections**))—
And oh yes, I am the **REAL** ((**Youthman Messenger**))—
Teaching working ways to be a ((**ceaseless**)) **rejuvenator**—
Here to arouse this world with ((**momentous revelations**))—
Here to uplift this planet with ((**lifelong salvations**))—
Here to help your body stay **disease-free and** ((**NEW**))—
Whereby your very **BEST years will be in FRONT of YOU**))) . . . .